Yoï

Yoï

THE REMARKABLE LIFE OF EDITH CORNELIA CROSSE (1877–1944)

For Lindsay, with best wishes

John Porter

John Porter

With an Introduction by Dacia Maraini

Matador
9 Priory Business Park,
Wistow Road, Kibworth Beauchamp,
Leicestershire. LE8 0RX
Tel: 0116 279 2299
Email: books@troubador.co.uk
Web: www.troubador.co.uk/matador
Twitter: @matadorbooks

ISBN 978 1789013 948

British Library Cataloguing in Publication Data.
A catalogue record for this book is available from the British Library.

Printed and bound by CPI Group (UK) Ltd, Croydon, CR0 4YY

Typeset in 11pt Aldine by Troubador Publishing Ltd, Leicester, UK

Matador is an imprint of Troubador Publishing Ltd

For Yve

Contents

Acknowledgements

Many people have been helpful in my research over a number of years. I would like to thank them all. If I have inadvertently omitted anyone, please accept my apologies.

Andrew Armour
James Bevan
Philippa Crosse
Deborah Jeffs
John P. Mahoney
Dacia Maraini
Mujah Maraini-Melehi
Silvester Mazzarella
Richard Porter
Alyson Price, Archivist, Harold Acton Library, The British Institute
of Florence
Benita Afan Rees
William Rees
Daria Rizzello
Ilaria B. Sborgi
Janet Tall of the South-West Heritage Service, Taunton
Fredric W. Wilson, The Harvard Theatre Collection, Houghton
Library, Harvard University
Marion Wolfert, Salt Lake City, Utah

YOÏ

Brian Wright

The staff of L'Archivio Contemporaneo "Alessandro Bonsanti",
Florence

My wife, Yve, for support and encouragement

Introduction by Dacia Maraini – My Grandmother, Yoï Crosse

Unfortunately, I never knew my father's mother, Yoï, a legendary figure in our family. When my father won a scholarship to go to Japan to study the Ainu people, I was barely a year old, and though I know she hugged me before we went, I cannot remember this.

I came to know Yoï through my father's stories and from the few surviving photographs of her, now reproduced by John Porter for the benefit of us all.

Yoï Pawlowska Crosse is a woman well worth remembering, I am sure of that. For many years, I took no interest in her, as might naturally be expected of a young girl obsessed with the future and with no interest in the past. But now that I have long outgrown the impatience and pride of youth, I find memory matters more than ever to me. As Bergson says, memory's deep roots form our conscience. And the significance of memory becomes more complex and profound than ever if we wish to resist the all-too-fashionable market culture of the present day in which even human beings can be bought and sold.

So, I believe it is important for us to recall from the past some strong and original figures that our over-hasty age has tried to consign to oblivion. One such person is unquestionably Yoï Pawlowska Crosse Maraini. She was an indomitable woman, romantically obsessed with love and travel, who during the late nineteenth and the early twentieth centuries paid a heavy price for her insistence on being fiercely independent at a time when many British and German women in particular did not flinch from uncomfortable and daring journeys through distant and self-contained and seldom penetrated parts of the world that often lacked roads and hotels; places then considered so remote that any woman who penetrated them was viewed with a mixture of anxiety and admiration.

Yoï was a brave woman who left her husband and children for the love of a diplomat called Roy who had passionately declared an eternal passion for her and threatened suicide if she did not come to live with him. She and Roy had previously shared a home in Rome, and when he was posted to Tehran, he expected her to join him. This she did, but only to find that all his protestations amounted to nothing. He changed his mind, leaving her without home, husband or children.

To understand how a beautiful young woman who left her husband for another man would have been judged and treated at the time, one could read *Effi Briest*, a novel written at about this time by the German novelist Theodor Fontane. Tolstoy's Anna Karenina was another woman who experienced much the same fate. Such women, judged irredeemably guilty, were forced to give up their homes and children, leaving them with nothing but the prospect of suicide if they insisted on trying to preserve the least scrap of honour.

Yoï, so suddenly and incomprehensibly abandoned by this apparently passionate lover, was indeed tempted to make an end of herself. But, saved by courage and her insatiable interest in the world combined with a passion for literature and writing, she decided to press on alone. Returning from Tehran to Rome, she faced up to the often considerable dangers of solitary travel at the time. Her initial journey from Rome to Tehran, when she was still full of hope, had taken fourteen days, as John Porter explains, requiring a succession of trains across Austria, Hungary and part of Russia as far as Baku on the west coast of the Caspian Sea, whence she took a boat to Persia. The way back, after rejection by her lover, was even longer and more hazardous, including a road blocked by fallen rocks, and boats confined to harbour by storms. She was forced to spend the nights in improvised shelters, her bed sometimes no more than a dirty carpet spread on the floor.

Yoï had no home or family to return to. She had very little money, and in England, the law prevented her even approaching her children. Luckily, her father, Andrew Frederick Crosse, had brought her up to be fearlessly independent and to make the best of every situation she might find herself in. Luckily too, she had inherited a talent for writing from her grandmother Cornelia, and this kept her company and helped protect her from depression and despair.

She wrote for the press, and, when able, also published books that contained nothing affected or conventionally "feminine". She described her travels with directness and transparency, fascinated by the amazing variety of the countryside and the different customs and particularities of the many peoples with whom she interacted. It is no surprise that her son Fosco became an ethnologist, inheriting his mother's passion for learning about unfamiliar peoples, something he passed on to me, together with a delight in reading and writing. As for Yoï, she never lost her anthropological curiosity, while her need to put down on paper what she saw and experienced on her travels helped her to survive.

Travel was always at the centre of her life, first from Tállya in Hungary where her father had bought some land and married a Hungarian-Polish wife, to London, and eventually Paris, Rome, Tehran and Florence. Travel brought her understanding and freedom. A freedom that sometimes cost her dear because travel in the early twentieth century was often no less uncomfortable than dangerous, but it also gave her the joy of making the world she discovered, in a small way, her own.

If Yoï had been a man, people would probably have carefully analysed what she wrote about travel. But since she was a woman her experiences came into the category of "eccentricities", anomalies that deviated from the normal, extravagances to be viewed with a degree of suspicion and disapproval. It is enough to read Ibsen's *A Doll's House* to understand what was expected of women at the time, even in the most enlightened and emancipated middle-class families. Even when she became a mother, a young woman was still treated as a child who needed control, direction and support. Lovingly administered perhaps, but certainly not with the respect that Ibsen's Nora required if she was to be accepted as a fully aware and responsible woman.

The young Yoï we see in one of the photographs, with her flimsy white dress, extremely long hair and angelic face, proves that at thirteen she was already a "romantic", in the sense that the German philosopher Fichte understood the term, to mean finite but at the same time reaching at least intermittently towards the infinite. Yoï's soft, ethereal dress and long, thick, almost fox-like hair bring to mind David Garnett's story *Lady into Fox*, in which, with loving admiration, Garnett claims that deep within herself every woman conceals the body and soul of a wild animal. Yet to me, Yoï is more reminiscent of a swallow than a fox. Her restlessness suggests that her fragility conceals a strength that will enable her to despise convention and rise as if on wings towards the unknown. I wonder if she knew Coleridge's poem *Farewell to Love*:

> '*Farewell, sweet Love! Yet blame you not my truth;*
> *More fondly ne'er did mother eye her child*
> *Than I your form. Yours were my hopes of youth,*
> *And as you shaped my thoughts, I sighed or smiled. . .*
> *To you I gave my whole, weak, willing heart.*'

Or the sad lines to which the same poet gave the title *Something Childish, but Very Natural*:

> '*But in my sleep to you I fly:*
> *I'm always with you in my sleep!*
> *The world is all one's own.*
> *But then one wakes, and where am I?*
> *All, all alone.*'

Lines which seem to me in tune with the period when Yoï was living and the passions she experienced.

She was saved by her natural vitality. A quality that did not exist in isolation but surfaced when she communicated with other people. And it was, in fact, in conversation with some young Italians that, after long sadness, she discovered love in the person of my grandfather Antonio Maraini, a talented young sculptor with modern ideas who, ignoring the conventions of his time, decided to marry this much-abused Englishwoman who had such a strongly individual personality.

It is a pity that Yoï, normally so sympathetic to people rejected by the world, should have been attracted to the fascism that ensnared Italy in her time. But as Porter explains, Mussolini was two-faced; on the one hand, he encouraged thugs who beat up those who did not share their views, while, on the other, he took trouble to present himself to the foreign press as a democratic lover of peace and dialogue. Yoï, securing an interview with him for an English weekly paper, fell into this trap, proving a generous and enthusiastic interviewer who allowed herself to be charmed. But this was the mid-1920s and fascism had not yet revealed its true face of racism, intolerance and misogyny.

Though he was still only a boy, Yoï's son Fosco had a better understanding than his parents of the perverse and dangerous factors that were developing inside this self-styled new socialism. This brought him into collision with his father. But not with his mother, which makes me think that Yoï was quicker than her husband to detect what lay behind the plausible expression on Mussolini's face. In any case, Fosco defied his parents to win an international scholarship that took him to Japan with his young Sicilian wife and newborn daughter – which was me. Both my parents – my mother, Topazia, no less than my father, Fosco – felt a need to get away from their family background and from the aggressive racism then beginning to raise its ugly head in Italy.

I remember that later, in our concentration camp in Japan, reduced to hungry skeletons and terrified by bombs and the violence of our guards, my father fell prey to an ominous presentiment. Almost in tears, he claimed that a letter sent by his mother had not reached us, presumably because the police had intercepted it. But later we heard that the day of his foreboding was the very day his mother, the sweet Yoï, had died.

Which is why, as an adult, I was never able to hug my fascinating grandmother, who had lived such a full and adventurous life and suffered so much but also found much in the world to love and write about. She had had to accept separation from the two children of her first marriage. But we should not forget that, even after her marriage to Antonio Maraini, she went back to England every year to see them, Wilma and Ifor, who never turned against her or rejected her but continued to return her love and hold her close in their thoughts for the rest of her life.

Dacia Maraini

(translated by Silvester Mazzarella)

Author's Introduction

Some years ago, while researching the life and family of Andrew Crosse (1784 – 1855), an early investigator of the new science of electricity, I came upon an announcement of his granddaughter Edith's marriage, which took place in London in 1896. At the time I took very little notice. It was obviously a "society" wedding, and I assumed that Edith Crosse was probably a typical lady of the time, leading a life of little excitement or interest. I imagined her doing little more than providing children to inherit the possessions and indulging in refined conversation over a cup of afternoon tea. However, as my research into the Crosse family continued I came upon further details of her life and gradually realised that my assumptions could hardly have been more mistaken.

This is her story.

A note on names and sources

If the reader is to keep track of the characters in any narrative, it is essential that their names are easy to remember and are used consistently. The subject of this book presents a problem – she was known at various periods of her life by a number of different names. She was baptised as *Kornelia Editha Crosse*, but later this became anglicised and altered to *Edith Cornelia Crosse*. Her first marriage changed her surname to *Buckley*, her second to *Maraini*, and she adopted the name *Yoï Pawlowska* for her early writings, *Pawlowska* being the feminine form of her mother's family name *Pawlowski*. After quite a lot of thought, I decided to refer to her throughout as *Yoï*. This was actually a nickname, but except on legal documents it was the name she used herself, and it is how she was known to family, friends and acquaintances. It is pronounced in a similar way to the names *Zoë* or *Joey*.

Yoï's second husband, Antonio Maraini, was always called *Nello* by Yoï and their family and friends, *Nello* being short for *Antonello*, the diminutive form of *Antonio*. However, I have generally referred to him as *Antonio*, except where *Nello* appears in quoted passages, as he was known as *Antonio* in the world outside his circle of friends and family. The family surname, *Maraini*, is pronounced with four distinct syllables with the stress on the third one: *Mar ah een ee*.

Pawlowska is pronounced as if it was spelt *Pavlovska*, and similarly, Yoï's daughter *Wilma*'s name should be pronounced *Vilma*.

Place names have changed over time and with changes in political systems. In passages quoted from contemporary documents, I have in general converted them to their modern form and spelling, so for example *Tokay* becomes *Tokaj*. However, where the place name is used in the title of a publication, for example, the *Llanelly Mercury*, I have kept the original spelling in order to make life easier for anyone who might wish to follow up the reference.

Both Yoï and her son Fosco wrote fictionalised accounts of their early years, with many personal names being changed. For example, the young Yoï appears as Anna in *A Child Went Forth;* Fosco becomes Clé in his *Case, amori, universi*. This causes obvious problems of separating fact and fiction. I have generally made an assumption that the emotional content of their accounts is fairly accurate but that locations and names are not to be relied upon unless backed up by other sources.

In quoted passages, square brackets are used to indicate where I have inserted text to clarify the meaning – for example, G[ordon] C[raig].

Family background

Even today, Broomfield, in the county of Somerset in the south west of England, is a very small village. There are only a few houses near the church, and a number of scattered farms. Broomfield is the highest settlement on the Quantock Hills, which form a low ridge from just north of the county town of Taunton to the Somerset coast between Bridgwater and Minehead. By the eighteenth century, the old mansion house of Fyne Court, Broomfield, had already been the home of the Crosse family for many generations and it was here that the best-known member of that family, Andrew Crosse,[1] was born in 1784.

Andrew was sent to school in Bristol and later went to Brasenose College, Oxford, where he graduated in 1806. He then returned to Fyne Court and devoted himself to the study of the new science of electricity. In 1809, he married Mary Ann Hamilton, whose family had property in Tiverton and Fermanagh. They had seven children in all, but three of them died in childhood.

In addition to his work as a local landowner and magistrate, Andrew Crosse gradually built up a national reputation as a scientist, although his Somerset neighbours were always very nervous about the experiments he carried out at Fyne Court, which sometimes gave rise to what they thought of as "thunder and lightning". Away from Somerset, his friends included many of those who were also carrying out pioneering work in understanding electricity – Sir Humphrey Davy and Michael Faraday among them.

Andrew's electrical experiments continued for years, and he was always adding to and improving his apparatus. At one time, he had nearly 500 metres of wire strung round the trees at Fyne Court to collect atmospheric electricity. His knowledge was put to practical use for medical purposes. People would go to Fyne Court to be electrified for paralysis and rheumatism, and in almost every case the effect was highly beneficial.[2]

Andrew Crosse's wife Mary Ann died in 1846. Four years later, at the age of sixty-six, he married again. His new bride was Cornelia Berkeley, who was considered to be a great beauty and was forty-three years younger than Andrew. While still a girl, she had been an enthusiastic follower of Andrew's scientific work and had kept a scrapbook of press cuttings of his work on electricity. The couple seem to have been devoted to one another. They loved to take long walks together over the Quantock Hills, and at Fyne Court Cornelia worked as Andrew's laboratory assistant and entertained many eminent people.

Andrew and Cornelia had three sons. The eldest, Andrew Frederick Crosse, was born at Fyne Court on 31 May 1852. He was baptised in the Church of St Mary and All Saints, Broomfield, on 11 July. His brother, Landor Richard, was born in 1854, and the youngest, Ormonde, in 1855. The three boys hardly knew their father, as Andrew Crosse died on 6 July 1855. He was seventy-one. Andrew's elder son from his first marriage, John, who had changed his surname to Hamilton in order to become his maternal uncle's heir, inherited the Fyne Court estate.

Cornelia Crosse and her three young sons now left Broomfield. They lived for a while at Comeytrowe House, just to the south of Taunton, and they were still there when, a few months after Andrew's death, a family friend, Sir Roderick Murchison, persuaded Cornelia to write a biographical memoir of her late husband. This was published in 1857 and proved very popular.

Some years later and now living in London at 32 Delamere Terrace, Paddington, Cornelia Crosse took up writing on a regular basis. She was a contributor to several journals:

Years went by without her writing more than an occasional magazine article, until her old and valued friend, George Bentley, persuaded her to write some reminiscences of the scientific and literary folk amongst whom she lived. These appeared in Temple Bar, *and met with so much approval that they were collected in 1892 into two volumes, and* Red Letter Days of My Life *are well-known among the most successful biographical works of the day… [She] was a contributor to the* Queen, *and at different times she has written for* Once a Week, Blackwood's Magazine, Chambers's Journal, *the* London Quarterly Review, *etc.*[3]

Cornelia's unmarried younger sister, Theresa Berkeley, lived with her and the three boys. Theresa looked after the running of their home so that Cornelia could concentrate on her writing. The family sometimes travelled abroad – the author H. Rider Haggard was later to remember meeting them on holiday at Dunkirk. He wrote:

Several of my elder brothers, particularly Jack and Andrew, and I, together with some other English boys, among whom were the sons of the late Andrew Crosse, the scientist, formed ourselves into a band and fought the French boys of a neighbouring lycée. These youths outnumbered us by far, but what we lacked in numbers we made up for by the ferocity of our attack. One of our stratagems was to stretch a rope across the street, over which the little Frenchmen, as they gambolled joyously out of school, tripped and tumbled. Then, from some neighbouring court where we lay in wait, we raised our British war-cry and fell upon them. How those battles raged! To this day I can hear the yells of "Cochons d'Anglais!" and the answering shouts of "Yah! Froggie, allez a votre maman!" as we hit and kicked and wallowed in the mire. At last I think the police interfered on the complaints of parents, and we were deprived of this particular joy.[4]

When the eldest of Cornelia's sons, Andrew Frederick Crosse, was thirteen, he attended Westminster School. He was admitted there on 15 June 1865 and left at Whitsun in 1867.[5] He developed an interest in chemistry, particularly metallurgy, at a comparatively early age. In the census taken on the night of 2 April 1871, Andrew is described as a "Student of Chemistry", aged nineteen. The other members of the family present that night were his mother Cornelia, his aunt Theresa Berkeley, his grandmother Cornelia Berkeley, and his two younger brothers Landor and Ormonde, who were both still at school. There were two servants: Hester Bishop, aged twenty-eight, and Esther Harris, aged twenty-nine.

Cornelia Crosse was a popular hostess, and many of London's literary figures were regular visitors to 32 Delamere Terrace. She was also a keen traveller. Over the years, her journeys took her to many European countries and on several occasions as far as Hungary to stay with friends there. Hungary at that time was still part of the Austrian Empire, although since 1867 it had been largely autonomous.

Like his mother, Andrew Frederick Crosse loved travelling. By 1875, he had already visited Norway, as well as the Austrian and Swiss Alps, and was still only twenty-three when in the June of that year he set out on a tour of Hungary and Transylvania. Much of his journey was on horseback, although sometimes he travelled in a traditional ladder-sided wagon drawn by a single horse over rough roads. Near Oravicza in Hungary (now Oravița in south-western Romania) he heard of a gold mine being run by an English gentleman and made arrangements to visit it. To his surprise, on meeting the Englishman and comparing notes, he found they had both been at Westminster School at the same time, although his new acquaintance, George Heath, had been some years senior to Andrew.

> ... *we had not known each other well; but meeting here in the wilds, we were as old familiar friends. He kindly insisted on my leaving the inn and taking up my quarters with him in his bachelor residence, which was in fact big enough to accommodate a whole form of Westminster boys.*[6]

Before leaving England, Andrew had been provided with various letters of introduction to friends and acquaintances of his mother, so towards the end of his trip he took the opportunity to stay at several *chateaux* and meet some of the nobility of the country.

> *For the time my wild rovings were over. The bivouac in the glorious forest and robber-steak cooked by the camp fire – the pleasures of "roughing it" – were exchanged for the charms of society.*[7]

Robber-steak consisted of bits of bacon, onion, and beef, seasoned with red pepper, and strung on sticks, and roasted over the fire, according to the author Bram Stoker in his best-known work *Dracula*.

In 1878, Andrew published an account of his travels under the title *Round About the Carpathians*, a fascinating account including local politics, folk customs, hunting, and the local mining industry. By the time the book appeared, Andrew had become a Fellow of the Chemical Society. Andrew's book does not tell us very much about events in his personal life, although he does admit to having an eye for the pretty girls of some of the villages on his route. He does not mention that on 30 September 1876 he was married, in Pressburg,[8] or Bratislava as it is today.

His bride, Emilia Pawlowski, was the daughter of Johann Pawlowski von Jaroslaw, a minor aristocrat of Polish origin who was now living in the Tokaj region of Hungary. The Pawlowski family originated in the region around Jaroslaw, in Galicia, in southern Poland. Emilia's grandfather, János Pawlowski, held the rank of *Ritter*, roughly the equivalent of *Knight* in English, or *Chevalier* in French. He was an official of the estate of Prince Esterházy at Eisenstadt, near Vienna. János's wife was born Franciska Stessel, and her family was also involved in the administration of the Esterházy estates. The composer Joseph Haydn, who was the Prince's *Kapellmeister*, or musical director, mentions Chief Cashier Stessel in a letter dated June 1798.[9]

János and Franciska Pawlowski had four children: two girls and two boys. The title of *Ritter* descended to the elder son, Alexander. He had a brilliant career as a lawyer, educator and administrator, eventually becoming Director of the prestigious *Theresianum* in Vienna, a military college that had been founded by the Empress Maria Theresa of Austria in 1751.

Alexander's younger brother, Johann, was also probably born at Eisenstadt. As an adult, Johann bought an estate near Tállya, in the Tokaj wine region of Hungary. He married Maria Winkler, whose family were Austrian in origin. On Alexander's death in 1882, the title of *Ritter* passed to Johann. Maria and Johann had four children: Emerentia, Emilia, Hedwig and Alexander.

Many years later, Andrew and Emilia's second daughter, Gabriella, wrote of the Pawlowski family and her parents' meeting:

> *They were Catholics and Polish nobles. When Frederick the Great, the Tsar of Russia, and Maria Therese agreed to partition Poland, the Pawlowskis' estate fell*

to Austria. To partly compensate them, they were given court appointments… Our grandfather, the Chevalier von Pawlowski, bought an estate near Tállya, not far from Tokaj, and there my father paid a visit and fell in love with my very lovely mother. German and French were their languages in common, for it took my father some years before he spoke some Hungarian – it is a difficult language. Of course my mother, like all continental children of good family, had to speak two or three languages.

The parents on both sides were much concerned and wished to know more of the families. In later years I heard how the letters of inquiry to embassies crossed on their way; eventually the arrangement was allowed when they heard that my father was of an old country family in Somerset and my mother of a noble Polish – now Austrian – family. There were three lovely daughters, all married, and a son, Alexander, the youngest child, who became equerry to the tragic Empress Elizabeth. In one salon we had a beautiful oil painting of her. I can never forget her lovely face. Her son Rudolf had been educated by my great uncle, who was director of the Theresianum, a military college for royalty and nobility founded by Maria Therese.[10]

It is very probable that Emilia and Andrew met while Andrew was staying with Baron and Baroness Vay at their château at Golop, just 3 km from Tállya. In his book, Andrew writes:

My first expedition to the Tokaj district was in the winter; I was then the guest of Baron V--, who has a charming château, surrounded by an English garden, in this celebrated place of vineyards.[11]

Another family friend was John Paget (1808 – 1892), the English agriculturist and writer on Hungary. He had graduated in medicine at Edinburgh University but never practised or used the title of doctor, though he further pursued the study of medicine in Paris and Italy. In Italy, he met the Baroness Polyxena Wesselényi, the widow of Baron Ladislaus Bánffy, and married her in 1837 in Rome. He devoted himself to the development of his wife's estates, at Gyéres, in Transylvania. He gained a high reputation as a scientific agriculturist and a beneficent landlord, introducing an improved breed of cattle and paying special attention to viniculture. Cornelia Crosse later wrote that she had met John Paget in

Budapest in 1876, which suggests that she probably visited Hungary for her son Andrew's wedding that September.[12]

After their marriage, Emilia and Andrew settled in Tállya, which is in Zemplén County in the northeast of Hungary and not far from Tokaj. Their daughter Gabriella later wrote:

> ... *my father bought a large estate to interest himself in growing grapes and making wine for export. He had of course a good agent and manager, and employed many men to cultivate the vines which grew on the hills some way from the town in which was our home, a large house in lovely gardens. At first we had governesses and later went to school.*[13]

The region was noted for the high quality of its wines, with Tállya itself producing some of the best. In his book, Andrew described in some detail the extremely labour-intensive processes that were involved:

> *Vineyards... can only be worked "intensively". Nothing requires more care and attention. To begin with, the aspect of the vine garden influences the quality of the wine immensely. Then there is the soil. The best is the plastic clay, which appears to be the product of the direct chemical decomposition of volcanic rock. This clay absorbs water but very slowly, and is, in short, the most favourable to the growth of the vine. As the vines are mostly on the steep hillsides, low walls are built to prevent the earth from being washed away. In the early spring one of the first things to be done is to repair the inevitable damage done by the winter rain or snow to these walls, and to clear the ditches, which are carefully constructed to carry off the excess of water. I should observe that in the autumn, soon after the vintage, the earth is heaped up round the vines to protect them from the intense cold which prevails here, and directly the spring comes, one must open up the vines again. In Tokaj the vines are never trellised, they are disposed irregularly, not even in rows – the better to escape the denudation of their roots by rain. Each vine is supported by an oak stick, which, removed in autumn, is replaced in spring after the process of pruning. When the young shoots are long enough they are bound to these sticks, and are not allowed to grow beyond them.*
>
> *No less than three times during the summer the earth should be dug up round the roots of the vine, and it is very desirable to get the second digging over before the harvest, for when harvest has once commenced it is impossible to get labourers at*

any price. The harvest operations generally begin at the end of June, and last six weeks… It is not till the third or fourth week in October that the vintage is to be looked for. It is not the abundance of grapes that makes a good year; the test is the amount of dried grapes, for it is to these brown withered-looking berries that the unique character of the wine is due. If the season is favourable, the over-ripe grapes crack in September, when the watery particles evaporate, leaving the raisin-like grape with its undissipated saccharine matter.

In order to make "Essenz", these dry grapes are separated from the rest, placed in tubs with holes perforated at the bottom. The juice is allowed to squeeze out by the mere weight of the fruit into a vessel placed beneath. After several years' keeping, this liquid becomes a drinkable wine, but of course it is always very costly. This is really only a liqueur. The wine locally called "Ausbruch" is the more generally known sweet Tokaj, a delicious wine, but also very expensive. It is said to possess wonderfully restorative properties in sickness and in advanced age.[14]

He also reported that 1876 had brought the worst of three successive bad harvests:

… a disastrous frost on the 19th of May in that year completely destroyed the hopes and prospects of the vine-grower.[15]

These accounts suggest that it might have been a rather courageous, or maybe foolhardy, move to start a new life as a wine producer at that time. However, he was young and ready for a challenge, and he threw himself enthusiastically into his new career.

Childhood in Tállya

Andrew and Emilia's first child was born on the 30 July 1877 and baptised in the Reform Church in Tállya just a month later, on 30 August. The baby's godparents were Baron and Baroness Vay. The priest made a note in the register that details of the baptism were passed to the Roman Catholic priest's office, as the mother was Roman Catholic. A later note adds that the father, as an English subject, protested at this because he said that according to English law all children have to be Anglicans. This, of course, was not strictly true.

In the church register, the parents' names are given as Pawlowski, Emilia, and Crosse, Endre. Andrew is described as an English landowner. The register shows that the baby was baptised Kornelia Editha. Later, this became anglicised to Cornelia Edith, and later still Edith Cornelia, but for most of her life she was known to both family and friends by her childhood nickname, Yoï. Four and a half years later, on 16 January 1882, Andrew registered Yoï's birth with the British Vice-Consul in Budapest. Here, her names were recorded as Cornelia Edith, and Andrew's rank or profession is "wine-grower".

Emilia and Andrew had three more children: Gabriella Mathild, born 23 May 1879, Alfred Cromwell, born 22 March 1882 and Wilhelmine Hedwig, born 7 May 1885. Each of the children was baptised at the Reform Church in Tállya, and in each case a note was made in the register about their mother being Roman Catholic. Alfred Cromwell Crosse's godfather was Alfred James Queckett, a solicitor from London who was visiting them at the time.

YOÏ

There are very few surviving records of the Crosse family's life in Tállya, but in a fragment written towards the end of her life, Yoï's sister Gabriella recalled the winters:

The standard rose trees are all wrapped in straw, tubs of oleanders are removed to cellars, and the jalousie (shutters) taken off the windows and stored away in their place; other glass windows are put up so that each window becomes double to keep out the cold. As soon as the snow begins, the Victoria carriage is put away and a big roomy sledge is used, drawn by two horses, with jingling bells.

The space between the two glass windows is about a foot and there, on the 6th of December, we were allowed to put a shoe for St. Nicholas to put presents and sweets in, for that is the saint's day. He has nothing to do with Christmas; the tree and gifts then are brought by angels. Christmas was kept as one of the two most important feasts of the year. No one was forgotten. The poor were remembered and the servants all had good presents. In the nursery we were kept out of the way, getting most excited, but interested meanwhile by fairy stories told us by our dear old nurse. The stories we most loved were those of Rinaldo, a robber chief who lived with his band in deep caves in the forest, where they had their horses and every comfort. Poor people were often helped; it was the rich who were robbed to help the poor. He was the continental Robin Hood and many were the great adventures of Rinaldo and his men.

At last we heard the longed-for tinkling of a bell: the big double-doors of several rooms between our day nursery and the salon were opened, and we rushed in to see the biggest and loveliest Christmas tree ever. So tall was it that its topmost branch bent down with a lovely angel hanging from it, with wings outspread. The heavier toys were on the carpet at its foot and we all had our heart's desire and great joy.

The salon was large, with handsome double-doors. There was something quite unique in it that no continental drawing rooms have: an English fireplace. My father had this built so as to have an open wood fire. He was thought to be very peculiar for doing this and endangering his home and family, but nothing went wrong. In one corner of the salon there was a tall white china fireplace with a mantelpiece of oak and fed through a small door in its side. Mother must have enjoyed all these preparations and gift giving, and we all do to this day. She was very loving and kind, especially to her one and only son, Alfred. It made her weep when she felt she must punish him; not that he was very naughty, but if he took an egg out of a bird's nest, that did anger her, for she loved birds and fed them in the winter.[16]

Years later, Yoï wrote a fictionalised account of her childhood, which was published under the title *A Child Went Forth*.[17] It is quite difficult to separate fact and fiction, but the book as a whole appears to be written very much from personal experience, and where it is possible to compare accounts of events with other sources, there is broad agreement.

Yoï spent much of her time with the servants and the villagers and spoke Hungarian as well as English. Her father, who was still only twenty-five, wanted Yoï to grow up like a boy and not to be frightened of anything.[18] At times, he did find it difficult to play the part of a more conventional parent:

> *"… it is time you went to school; you must learn to be like other little girls and not such a tomboy."*
>
> *"But, Father, I don't like lessons."*
>
> *Her father was very grown up: he said sententiously:*
>
> *"We all have to do a great many things we do not like." Then he laughed out loud and wondered if every parent felt foolish when he talked platitudes to his child.*[19]

But soon her mother came in and took her through the village to see the schoolmaster:

> *They went out of the gate together and hand in hand down the street, passing houses hidden, as those in the East, by high walls and trees. Then they came to a street of very small houses all thatched with straw instead of being covered with shingles as the better houses were; they were painted with bright bands of colour and, like all the other houses, had their gable ends to the street. Each house had a long seat by the gate. Then they came to an open space with a well in the middle of it.*
>
> *… The school-house was a small, low building; it had a door in the middle and a window on either side higher up than the door. It was one of those houses which look like faces when children draw them in a book. Two chimneys at each end were the long ears listening to the chirping of many little birds.*[20]

Yoï soon settled in at school, and as her father was quite insistent that she should be brought up to be independent and fearless, she walked alone to and from school each day. In spite of Emilia's anxiety, Andrew set Yoï Sunday morning tasks to strengthen her nerves, such as climbing up one side of a stepladder, over the top, and down the other side. Emilia would have preferred to have taken Yoï to Mass with her, but this was not to be.

Yoï gradually became aware that her family were not like others around them – for example:

> ... *her mother was not like the mothers of the other children – she was dressed daintily, her hat was pretty too – she looked like a young girl. The mothers of the other children were all women of the village – they were not lovely, nor did they wear pretty hats, only handkerchiefs tied on their heads.*[21]

For years, Yoï's life was very settled, revolving around school and home. The tension over religion that was present when her baptism was registered was always there just below the surface, but her father's will seems to have prevailed in this as in a number of other matters. Emilia had promised him that Yoï would not be given any religious education until she was old enough to know what religion meant.

From time to time, there was talk of sending Yoï away to school in England, but her mother insisted that she would be better off staying there in Tállya – that she loved the village and its people and that the shock of being uprooted would be too much for her. However, Yoï was often in trouble – playing truant to go swimming with the village children, or fighting with a boy who had been bullying a smaller Jewish boy.

In *A Child Went Forth* she tells of a social call she and her mother paid on the old doctor. It was a very hot day and the adults talked endlessly, so she wandered out into the garden, where she discovered a water butt. She was too hot, so she took all her clothes off and climbed in, only to find that it was too deep to touch the bottom and that she could not get out. So she shouted until she was rescued. Her father later gave her a good telling-off – after all, she might have drowned – but she indignantly complained that she didn't know it was naughty – no one had ever specifically told her not to take off her clothes and climb into a water butt.[22]

The gypsy music of the country made a lasting impression on Yoï and her sister Gabriella, who was later to write:

> *Outside every town and near villages there would be a gypsy encampment, and amongst them a number of men who played violins. They played at feasts and dances, and then the harvest was over and the last of the grapes brought in. Such music! The joy and brightness of it made the heart light and the feet move. The csardas was irresistible, but when they played sad music it tore your heart with its exquisite pathos. Many years later in London, when my eldest sister [Yoï] and I, then just over 20, were lunching at the Carlton [Hotel], a gypsy band was playing Hungarian music in their national costume. But having heard that they dread crossing the sea because it might have a bad effect on their ability to play, I told my sister that I would test them. I wrote in Hungarian on the back of the menu card: "Please play for us Hirlamzo Balston". That was a lovely sad song about Lake Balaton in Hungary. There was great excitement and confabulation. In a few moments they played – and how they played! When they finished, they all stood up and bowed towards our table. Of course we sent them a nice tip, and when we rose to leave they again stood up and bowed to us. A lovely little adventure, so pleasant to remember. The strange and wonderful thing about these gypsy musicians is that they know nothing of written music; all is by ear, learned and passed on from father to son.*[23]

In about 1888, Andrew began to hear worrying reports of an outbreak of phylloxera in the Tokaj vineyards. Phylloxera is caused by a tiny sap-sucking insect that feeds on the roots of grapevines. Since the adult female deposits 500 to 600 eggs, and as soon as the young hatch they begin to feed, this pest could quickly ruin the wine production of an entire region. Anxiously, Andrew monitored its spread. The harvest that year was unaffected, but there was a feeling that the future might bring disaster for them all, landowners and workers alike:

> *After a long winter, bitterly cold, gloomy, and often wet, came a hot spring and a drought. The harvest threatened to be a bad one, and the vines were not doing well. There was much poverty and sorrow.*[24]

By 1889, it became only too clear that the phylloxera was approaching Tállya even more quickly than they had expected. Andrew and Emilia faced ruin. It was decided that Yoï would go to England to live with her grandmother and attend school there. The rest of the family would also have to move, but they hoped to return to Tállya one day. Gradually, Yoï got used to the idea, but she was still very apprehensive about such an immense change.

The vintage that autumn turned out to be worse than anyone had feared. In London, *The Times* reported:

> *... in Tokaj (two-thirds of this splendid vineyard have been destroyed by the phylloxera) there was but a small yield of little value, and the wet autumn has prevented the grapes from being converted into raisins, from which the highest class Tokaj is drawn.*[25]

The following year, an outbreak of fire added to the despair in all the local villages. The town of Tokaj itself was almost completely destroyed.[26] Tállya fared better, but even so, many houses were damaged.

Finally, the time came for Yoï to leave for England. She visited friends and family to say a sad goodbye, wondering if she would ever see them again. Her father was travelling with her as far as Vienna where she would join her cousins who were themselves going on to London, in the care of their governess. She was driven to the station, tearfully said goodbye to her mother, climbed aboard the train and watched sadly as Tállya slowly vanished in the distance. She was still only twelve years old and about to start a new life in a strange country.

Life in London

To a young girl who was used to running free in a Hungarian village, fashionable London must have come as a great shock. Her grandmother Cornelia lived at 32 Delamere Terrace, Paddington, which had been built some sixty years earlier as part of a development running westwards from Little Venice alongside the canal. From the start, the area had attracted a wide mix of residents. Robert Browning's sister-in-law Arabel Barrett was one, and Robert Browning himself lived nearby in Warwick Crescent between 1862 and 1887. He was an old acquaintance of Cornelia's and had visited Fyne Court on several occasions.[27] Edmund Gosse's family, at number 29, were particular friends of Cornelia and her sister Theresa. He was a translator at the Board of Trade, a poet, and had lectured on English literature at Trinity College, Cambridge, from 1885 to 1890. He was later to become librarian to the House of Lords.[28] Currently, he was working on the first translation of Henrik Ibsen's play *Hedda Gabler*. He and his wife had two daughters. The older one, Emily, was the same age as Yoï, while Laura was three years younger.

The only record we have of life at number 32 Delamere Terrace is from the census of 5 April 1891. Yoï's grandmother, Cornelia Crosse, was shown as head of the family and described as a widow aged sixty-four and living on her own means. Yoï's uncle, Ormonde Crosse, was thirty-six, single and described as a tutor. Cornelia's sister and Yoï's great-aunt, Theresa Berkeley was fifty-three, single and living on her own means. There were two servants: housemaid Emily Crook, eighteen, and the cook, Ada Ward, twenty-two. Yoï herself was thirteen and described as a scholar. Her name was recorded as "Edith C. Crosse" and her place of birth as Hungary, but with a note to say she was a British subject.

Far away in Hungary, Yoï's father, Andrew, was facing the total failure of the Tokaj region's wine production. He now decided upon a complete change of occupation. Gold had been discovered in South Africa, near Johannesburg, some five years earlier. The rapidly expanding goldfields needed technical people such as himself, and he planned to try his luck there. He left Tállya and travelled across Europe to England. Emilia and the three youngest children stayed in Tállya.

On 23 January 1891, Andrew sailed alone from Southampton on board the Union Lines steamer *Pretoria*,[29] bound for Cape Town and the goldfields of Johannesburg in the Transvaal. He remained there until the following spring, arriving back in London on 11 April 1892 on the *Dunottar Castle*[30] and then travelling on to Tállya. From here, he wrote to his mother, describing his welcome:

> *Emily and the children & several friends came to meet me at Szerencs midday Sunday. The children are all very well. Emily will be all the better for a change. When we came to the town all the fire brigade turned out to meet me. Half the town was there – they were so glad to see me, many of them cried as they knew I was going so soon. I never saw people who were really so sorry and on the other hand so glad to see me.*[31]

Gabriella later wrote of the occasion:

> *… my father returned from Africa. There were great rejoicings, and then great sorrow at the prospect of leaving Hungary – such parties and farewells, visiting relatives, great preparations and packings. To my mother it was a profoundly sad and moving matter. She spoke French and German, as well as Hungarian of course, but no English. One day when busy packing she called me aside and said, "You are now twelve; I can trust you to do what I ask. Here is a little velvet bag, filled with soil from our garden here, Hungarian earth. If by any chance I die in Africa, see to it that this little bag is thrown by you into my grave on top of my coffin."*[32]

On their long journey, the family stopped for a few days in Budapest, then later in Vienna, and Poszony (now Bratislava), where they stayed with Emilia's mother. Finally, they reached Vlissingen, where they took the overnight boat to England:

> *We were on our way to Flushing [Vlissingen], where we arrived at night to cross to England. Before it was too dark we were much amused to see little carts with cans of milk, etc., being drawn by large dogs; we thought these folk must be very frugal to make dogs work.*
>
> *… What a strange and other world it seemed, this England. We crossed at night and went straight to town, to the house of our English grandmother. It was a large house: she had her sister Theresa Berkeley and her son Ormonde living with her, but there seemed plenty of room for us all.*[33]

Yoï and her family were now together again, and for some weeks they all enjoyed life in London.

> *We were taken to see many wonderful things suitable for the young. There was a show going on at Earls Court called Venice: gondolas on canals and a small-scale Venice. Then we were taken to see Buffalo Bill. There were bright red coaches drawn by mules or horses, and the men used long whips in the wild and woolly west manner.*[34]

After five or six weeks in London, on 2 June, Andrew, Emilia and the three youngest children went to the East India Dock Basin, Blackwall, and boarded the Castle Line's steamer *Hawarden Castle*.[35] The family was going to start a new life in Africa.

One wonders whether Yoï was offered the choice of staying in London or going with the others to South Africa. Whatever the options, she stayed on at 32 Delamere Terrace.

The *Hawarden Castle* reached Madeira on 8 June and then continued to Cape Town, which was reached on 22 June. The family then set out across southern Africa to Johannesburg. But within less than six months of their landing in Africa, tragedy struck the young family. Emilia died, in Johannesburg, on 15 November 1892. She was only thirty-eight. The announcement appeared in London a few days later in *The Times*:

DEATHS

On the 15th Nov. at Johannesburg, South Africa, EMILY, wife of ANDREW F. CROSSE, Esq., daughter of the late Johann Ritter Pawlowski von Jaroslaw, of Tállya, Hungary.[36]

At her mother's funeral, Gabriella dutifully threw the little bag of Hungarian earth into the grave on top of the coffin.

Within less than two years, Yoï had been uprooted from her beloved Tállya, had had to adjust to a completely different way of life in London without her parents and siblings, been briefly reunited with her family, and almost immediately lost her mother forever. We can only imagine what effect this had on her. Although she was later to write frankly about various other periods of her life, she never seems to have done so about her teenage years. Perhaps it was all just too painful.

A few doors along from Cornelia Crosse's house in Delamere Terrace there was a Home for Trained Nurses. The assistant supervisor there was a friend of the family, Frances Charlotte Jennings. She now resigned her position and made the long journey to Johannesburg to become housekeeper to Andrew and his young family. Three years later, Frances and Andrew married in Cape Town, on 17 October 1895.[37]

Exactly what formal schooling Yoï received is not clear, but she was certainly encouraged by her grandmother to read widely, and in later life her knowledge of a remarkable range of literature is apparent in her own writing. As she grew older, she would certainly have met very many interesting and stimulating people, as her grandmother loved entertaining. But on 2 March 1895, when Yoï was still only seventeen, her grandmother Cornelia died. Mrs Alec Tweedie (*née* Ethel Brilliana Harley) contributed an obituary to *The Queen* magazine in which she described Cornelia as:

> *… a remarkable woman. She was a brilliant conversationalist, and a delightful addition to a dinner party. Nothing bored her more than music, which, she said, "spoils conversation," for although fond of art, and an admirer of poetry, of which her husband had some gift, she did not possess a musical ear, and disliked it rather than otherwise. She was an excellent hostess, and had that happy knack of making everyone feel at home and at their ease, and in former years entertained very largely; even latterly she was always surrounded on Sunday afternoons by numerous*

interesting folk, who were sure of a pleasant hour when they repaired to Delamere Terrace.

She was a devoted mother and grandmother, and her death will be a great loss to her family, more particularly to her sister, who has lived with her for many years. Since Mrs Crosse took to more serious literary work, Miss Berkeley kept the house, and relieved her of many household cares; consequently the handsome authoress was able to work in her little room upstairs in peace and quiet. Mrs Crosse spent all her morning in her study, and in the afternoon was able to pay or receive visits; while in the evening nothing delighted her more than a quiet rubber of whist.[38]

And *The Times* said of Cornelia:

She was a woman of remarkable social charm and sympathetic intelligence, knew a good story when she met with one, and could repeat it, either in conversation or in writing, with excellent effect.[39]

Eight months later, on 27 November 1895, the following announcement appeared in the *South Wales Daily Post*:

The engagement is announced of Mr James F. Buckley, Bryncaerau, Llanelli, eldest and only surviving son of the late Mr James Buckley, J.P. counties of Carmarthen and Brecon, D.L. county of Carmarthen, and High Sheriff 1895, to Miss Edith Crosse, eldest daughter of Mr Andrew Crosse of Johannesburg, South Africa and grand-daughter of the late Mr Andrew Crosse, JP of Fyne Court, Somersetshire.[40]

Still only eighteen years old, Yoï was engaged to be married.

Mrs James Buckley

Yoï's fiancé was a twenty-seven-year-old barrister and company director named James Buckley. The Buckleys were originally weavers from Lancashire, but James's great-grandfather, also called James Buckley, had become an itinerant Methodist preacher. His circuit had taken him to Llanelli, Carmarthenshire, towards the end of the 18th century. Here he had married Maria, the daughter of Henry Child, a local maltster and brewer, and the couple lived in a number of places in England and Wales before finally returning to Llanelli. James and Maria's son, another James, took over the Childs' brewery together with his brother, Henry. The business was very successful, and the family gradually became quite wealthy. In 1866, James Buckley bought the estate of Bryncaerau, on the northern outskirts of Llanelli, for his son, yet another James, who was about to be married to Marianne Hughes of Brecon. An Italianate mansion designed by J. B. Wilson, sometimes known as Bryncaerau Castle, had been built by 1886. It is now Parc Howard Museum and Art Gallery.

Marianne and James's first child was born at Bryncaerau on 12 February 1869 and named James Francis Hughes Buckley. Another son, Joseph, was born in 1870, followed by three girls, Blanche, Gwladys and Katherine. The two sons, James and Joseph, were sent as boarders to Christ College, Brecon. Later, James went to Rugby School, and then to Oriel College, Oxford, where he graduated in 1892. He was called to the Bar at the Inner Temple in 1894. His mother died in June that same year. James was by now the only surviving son, as his younger brother Joseph had died in 1890.

The family brewery was converted to a joint stock company in December 1894. Then in 1895 the elder James Buckley became High Sheriff of Carmarthenshire but died in September following a leg injury. As heir to his father's business interests, James Buckley was now an extremely eligible bachelor and would have been very welcome in London society. We do not know exactly how Yoï and James met, although it would probably have been at a social occasion of some sort. Yoï had lost her grandmother earlier that year, James had lost his father – perhaps they were able to be of comfort to each other. Their engagement was announced only two months after his father's death.

The marriage took place at Trinity Church, Paddington, on 21 April 1896. The *Llanelly Mercury* reported:

> *The church was crowded as family and guests arrived to celebrate what was a 'fashionable assembly' at the marriage of James Francis Hughes Buckley of Bryn y Caerau, Carmarthenshire and Miss Edith Cornelia Crosse. At 2.15 p.m. the bride entered the church leaning on the arm of her uncle Mr Ormonde Crosse. She wore a dress of white duchesse satin trimmed with orange blossoms, white feather and chiffon, her veil was fastened with a diamond tiara which the groom had given her… There were seven bridesmaids including, Miss Lily Buckley, Miss Rose Buckley, Miss Gwyn Jeffreys and Miss Cowell. Later in the day the young couple left for Paris en route to South Africa where they spent their honeymoon.*[41]

Yoï and James returned from Paris and boarded the Castle Line steamer *Tantallon Castle* at Southampton in time for its departure at 4.30 pm on 2 May. Already on board were several hundred military personnel of various ranks, including Lieutenant-Colonel R. S. Baden-Powell of the 13th Hussars, who was later to become famous as the founder of the Boy Scout movement. On the passenger list, Yoï and James are recorded as James F. Buckley, twenty-seven, gentleman, and Mrs Buckley, twenty-three, although in reality Yoï was still only eighteen. The ship called at Madeira on 6 May and reached Cape Town early on 19 May 1896.

At this time, Yoï's father, Andrew, was working in Johannesburg as a metallurgist, trying to develop improved methods for the extraction of the gold from its ore. By now, Yoï's sister Gabriella was seventeen, her brother

Alfred was fourteen, and her youngest sister, Wilhelmine Hedwig, was eleven. The 1,500 km journey by rail from Cape Town to Andrew's home in Johannesburg would have taken Yoï and James about thirty hours. The line in places reached an altitude of 1,066 metres before descending again to cross the vast expanse of the semi-desert known as the Great Karoo. Johannesburg itself had seen a phenomenal growth and transformation over the short period it had been in existence. Just a few years before Yoï and James's visit, *The Times* had printed a fairly detailed description of the growing city:

> *On the 20th of September, 1886, the Witwatersrand district was declared a public goldfield, and from that date the history of Johannesburg begins. For some months the town was known as Ferreira's Camp and the Natal Camp, and it was not till perhaps March last that the present town of Johannesburg became recognised as the central point of the goldfields of the district. From that date the growth of the town has been almost unprecedented. In almost every instance of the uprising of a digging town we find that a canvas town existed for many months, if not years, before permanent buildings were put up … At Johannesburg it is otherwise. The buildings are permanent and solid; most, of course, of iron, but many of brick, and others of substantial stone. The streets and squares are well laid out and even now the gaps existing between the various buildings are few and far between. Large hotels exist which equal in accommodation anything in South Africa. Warehouses are full of all that can be obtained even in Cape Town. A theatre, rough it is true, but of considerable capacity, is in full working order. Four banks are at work. Three newspapers are published every other day. Large public buildings are laid out, and shortly to be erected. Two clubs are already built to meet the requirements of social life. A large hall of worship for the use of members of the Church of England is on the verge of completion, and Wesleyan, Roman Catholic, and Dutch reformed churches are already built. Ministers of religion are already appointed to their several flocks, and schools are being rapidly organised for the comparatively few children who live in Johannesburg.*[42]

Remarkably, all these developments had taken place before the rail link to Cape Town was completed. It opened in 1892, just four years before Yoï and James Buckley's visit. They stayed in South Africa for a few months, arriving back in London on 1 August 1896.[43]

By 1899, Yoï and James were living in the Buckley family home of Bryncaerau, Llanelli. Yoï and James's first child, Wilma Susan Morwen Buckley, was born there on 12 November 1899. On her birth record, James's occupation is given as "barrister", but since his father's death in 1895 he had been increasingly involved in the family business: Buckley's Brewery.

Just a month or so before Wilma's birth, on 11 October 1899, war had officially been declared between Britain and the Boers in southern Africa. The causes of the war were complex, but they included a clash between imperial and republican political ideals as well as conflict over the goldfields of the Transvaal. The British Government hoped to unite South Africa under British Imperial rule, while the two Boer republics (the Orange Free State and the Transvaal, or South African Republic) wanted to keep their independence. Conflicts over access to the goldfields and the transport systems linking them to the Cape added to the tension.

By December 1899, the British Government had realised that they had severely underestimated their enemy and that more men would be needed than were available in the standing army. They appealed for volunteers to join the newly created Imperial Yeomanry. Officers and men were to bring their own horses, clothing and saddlery. The government would provide arms, ammunition, camp equipment and transport. The men were to be dressed in Norfolk jackets, of woollen material of neutral colour, breeches and gaiters, lace boots, and felt hats, although strict uniformity of pattern was not insisted upon. After a short period of training, they were shipped off to South Africa.

James Buckley was typical of many of his class in raising a local detachment of Yeomanry, and in June the local paper reported his growing involvement with military matters:

> *Hundreds of people turned out at the People's Park on Monday to give a send-off to the newly formed detachment of the Pembrokeshire Yeomanry. The spectacle of local men attired in the uniform of cavalry soldiers was a novel one and accounted for the attraction of so many people. It was only recently that Lieutenant James F. Buckley of Bryncaerau Castle, inaugurated the movement in Llanelli which has now culminated in the formation of a detachment of yeomanry, and it is surprising that so many should have responded to his invitation in so short a time. The men*

met on horseback in the Bryncaerau grounds and afterwards marched to the Town Hall Square, where they were photographed, before proceeding to Tenby, where they will take part in the annual training, which extends over a period of ten days. The men in their elaborate accoutrements, and mounted on spirited animals, presented a very smart appearance, and their progress through the principal streets of the town created no little interest and won the admiration of all who saw them. A little way beyond Carmarthen, they were met by Lieut. Buckley, who rode with them down to Tenby.[44]

By early 1901, things were not going well with the war in South Africa, and a second wave of recruitment was undertaken by the Government. On 20 April 1901, James was one of many on board the *Tantallon Castle* when she sailed from Southampton under Captain H. D. Travers. But on 7 May the ship ran aground in thick fog on Robben Island, just 7 km from Cape Town:

The Tantallon Castle struck at 4 o'clock, while going dead slow owing to the fog. A passenger states that she grounded only on the sandy portion of the island. The shock was light and the vessel is quite undamaged. The utmost order prevailed. Signals were made for assistance, and the tugs arrived at 5 o'clock. The passengers were easily transhipped, as the sea was very calm. The mails are now being transferred, and it is hoped that the vessel will be saved. The fog began this morning and the captain immediately slowed down and took continual soundings, which were satisfactory. Nevertheless he decided to anchor, and was on the point of doing so when the vessel grounded. The passengers for Cape Town have been landed and the through passengers have been transferred to the Saxon.[45]

But just two days later, the situation had deteriorated considerably:

Avondale Castle and Raglan Castle returned from Tantallon. All hope is abandoned of getting her off. Impossible to board this morning owing to heavy sea breaking over her. Every prospect of bad weather. Captain Travers and 20 of crew in tug standing by. Stokehold full of water, consequently salving cargo almost impossible owing want appliances.

    … the passengers of the Tantallon Castle… presented an address to Captain Travers expressing their warm sympathy with him at the mishap, testifying to

the great care exercised in the navigation, and appreciating the splendid discipline
shown after the ship had grounded.[46]

A Court of Enquiry subsequently found Captain Travers guilty of a grave error of judgement but considered that the circumstances of the wreck and his meritorious record did not justify his suspension. The other officers were acquitted of all blame.[47]

By the end of 1901, the war in Africa was going Britain's way, but it was not until the end of May 1902 that a formal peace agreement was signed. James was by now Captain Buckley, the promotion having being announced in the *London Gazette* in March.[48] He did not leave for home until the end of the year, sailing from Cape Town on the steamship *Norman* on 17 December. The ship arrived at Southampton on 3 January 1903.[49]

Yoï's father and the other members of his family had returned to England for the duration of the Boer War. As late as January 1909, his address was 41 Oxford Terrace, Hyde Park, London.[50] Andrew and his second wife, Frances Charlotte, did not return to Johannesburg until July 1909.[51]

Scandal

James and Yoï, with their young daughter, Wilma Susan, now settled down to married life. They lived partly at Castell Gorfod, near St Clears in Carmarthenshire, but mainly at their town house at 19 Norfolk Street, Park Lane, in one of the most fashionable parts of London. It was there on 16 October 1904 that Yoï gave birth to a son. They named him Gabriel James, but he was always known as Ifor.

Throughout the next few years, James Buckley was taking a very active part in running the family brewing concern, and was frequently away on business trips to Llanelli. With the two children in the capable hands of the domestic staff, Yoï had little with which to occupy herself. When James was at their home in London, they had the usual round of social engagements, but by the end of 1908, Yoï was thirty-one years old, lively and intelligent – and almost certainly bored. It was in December of that year that she first met the man who was to completely change her life.

Known as Roy to his friends, and renowned for his good looks, Sir Coleridge Arthur Fitzroy Kennard was the son of the late Hugh Coleridge Downing Kennard, of the Grenadier Guards, and his wife Helen, *née* Wyllie. Young Roy Kennard had been created the first Baronet Kennard, of Fernhill, Southampton on 11 February 1891 when he was only five years old. The baronetcy had originally been intended for his grandfather and namesake Coleridge Kennard, co-founder of the *Evening News*, but grandfather Kennard had died before it could be awarded.

Roy had never known his father, as Hugh Kennard had died when Roy was still a baby. His mother, Helen Kennard, remarried when Roy was ten years old. Her second husband was James Carew, M P for the Southern Division of County Meath, Ireland. Helen had been a great friend of Oscar Wilde, and it was her donation of £2,000 that later enabled the young Jacob Epstein to be commissioned to create a monument for Wilde's grave in Paris.

In 1904, Helen Carew commissioned the French painter Jacques-Emile Blanche to produce a painting of her son. Blanche posed him on a sofa at his studio in Auteuil and called the picture *Sir Coleridge Kennard Sitting on the Sofa*. However, when she saw the finished work, Roy's mother strongly disapproved of this portrait, which shows him as a young dandy – a rather stereotypical image of an English aristocrat. Her objections prompted the painter to give the work a new title when he exhibited it some years later. He called it *The Portrait of Dorian Gray*. It is not known whether Helen Carew considered this an improvement.

Roy Kennard met Yoï for the first time in December 1908, when he was twenty-three and she was thirty-one. He seems to have become completely infatuated with her and almost immediately started trying to persuade her to leave her husband and children and elope with him. Helen Carew was not going to stand for this sort of thing. At the time, Roy was a fairly new recruit to the Diplomatic Service, working as an attaché in the Foreign Office. Mrs Carew had friends in high places, including the Foreign Office, and on 13 March 1909 she went to see them.

Her visit was successful – in an attempt to put a stop to the relationship, Roy was told by his superiors that he was immediately to be transferred to Rome. By the end of March, he was there. From his flat in Rome, he telegraphed and wrote to Yoï constantly, asking her to go away with him and telling her how much he hated the Diplomatic Service. The worry and distress made Yoï ill. She developed a high fever and was attended by a doctor over a period of about three weeks.

Finally, in May 1909, she made her decision. She told her daughter, Wilma, who was still only nine years old, 'When you wake up tomorrow, I will not be here.' On 15 May, she went as far as Paris, where she seems to have hesitated about what to do next. Roy continued to write and telegraph almost daily. On 31 May, he wrote:

If you still hesitate, if you decide to go back – and what good can it do – I must be sure that you will come in July… If you think for a moment that from Wales or London before starting you will think and write again in doubt, I shall come now.[52]

Yoï answered that she did not want to go away with him just then, though she did want to be with him. She said she was too ill to decide at that moment and that she wanted at any rate to go back to England first. She also explained that she had no money of her own, although she did have some money coming to her and would use this to settle a few debts she had incurred.

Roy replied at length setting out his own financial position, even sending an accountant's statement. All he had of his own was a legacy of about £10,000 and the money held by the Kennard trustees, about £50,000, which he could not touch until his 25th birthday on 12 May 1910. Meanwhile, he would only be receiving an allowance from the trustees. He explained that any other expectations he had depended entirely on the goodwill of his mother and grandmother, and these would almost certainly be sacrificed if he went away with Yoï.

Yoï was taken ill again in Paris at the end of May, having a very high fever, and was attended by a doctor for a fortnight. Meanwhile, Roy kept up his bombardment by telegram.

On 5 June, he wrote:

Tell me what the doctors say, how your head is and the fever… when it goes down. You must put out of your head any idea of going back to London.

On 7 June:

I must come – do not let it be otherwise. Tell me that when you are strong enough to move that we will go together.

On 8 June:

If you go back now I shall torture myself to death. I have reached and known all that I can stand.

On 9 June, he wired:

> *Another period of waiting would kill us both. It could bring no other decision but only pain again and I cannot be without you... we leave everything to gain everything. I will hold you – do not fear. But say that you will come – that you will give up fighting when I am there so that we may meet at last on Saturday and go.*

Yoï replied continually that she must go back to England first and that she was too ill to decide to go away then. By Saturday 12 June, she had been in bed for fourteen days and was very weak. On this day, Roy arrived in Paris and insisted that they should go away at once, saying that he would not live if she did not go with him then. In spite of Yoï's illness, and her strong reservations, the following day they left Paris for Munich and then on 16 June they arrived in Vienna. Roy insisted on posting the letters that Yoï had written to her husband and friends, as well as the letters he had written to his mother, to tell them all that they had gone away together.

A few days later, they had arrived at the mountain resort of Tatra-Lomnitz (now known as Tatranská Lomnica) in the Western Carpathian Mountains. Here, Yoï became so depressed at what she had done that she attempted suicide, taking an overdose of sulphonal, a chemical compound that at the time was in use as a hypnotic drug, but has since been superseded by newer and safer sedatives. The local doctor was called and succeeded in saving her.

Roy now received a sternly worded telegram from Sir Charles Hardinge of the Foreign Office, demanding that he return to London. Roy insisted on Yoï making the decision – he was himself toying with the idea of going to somewhere far away from Europe. Yoï felt that they should return to London "as a matter of honour" to face the consequences of their actions. They arrived back in London on 11 July and took a room together at the Russell Hotel.

Over the next few days, Roy had a series of interviews at the Foreign Office with Sir Charles Hardinge and other officials. At some of these, a representative of Mrs Carew's solicitors, Lewis & Lewis, was also present; at others, his mother's friend Robert Ross, the art critic and sometime lover, and later the literary executor, of Oscar Wilde.

On 13 July, Messrs Lewis & Lewis wrote to Yoï's solicitor saying that Sir Coleridge Kennard was to be sent to Tehran, and that

> *… under the circumstances he is desirous of doing everything that is honourable and fair towards the lady… We may add that it is in consequence of orders from the Foreign Office that he is compelled to go abroad and leave the lady, for whom he entertains great affection.*

Yoï was told both by Roy himself and also by Robert Ross that unless he did as the Foreign Office demanded he would be dismissed…

> *… in such a way as no one had ever been dismissed before, and that the consequence would be permanent disgrace, such that he could never live in England or meet English people.*

However, they both assured her that when the divorce case came on, he would at once be allowed to leave the Diplomatic Service. Messrs Lewis & Lewis also wrote to Yoï's solicitor telling him…

> *… clearly to understand that Mrs Carew will not stand quietly by and see her son denuded of his fortune and made the subject of a public scandal, without in every possible way and at all times taking steps to expose the circumstances and the mode in which her son has been treated.*

On the morning of 23 July, Yoï, still very weak and ill, left London on the way to the spa town of Bad Ems, near Koblenz in Germany, to take the cure ordered by her doctor. She stopped at Brussels on the first night of her journey. That same afternoon, Roy left London and telegraphed to Yoï to meet him that night at the station in Brussels. She did so and travelled from there with him as far as Nuremberg. She then begged him that, if he had any doubt in his mind that they might have made a mistake, he would let her try to get her husband to be reconciled to her and let her return to him. She told Roy that if he would not let her attempt this now then she could certainly never attempt it afterwards. Roy's response was that if she even thought of such a thing, he would kill himself.

He would carry out the Foreign Office's instructions to move to

Tehran and wait for the divorce case to take place. His understanding was that his being named as co-respondent would result in his automatic dismissal from the Diplomatic Service, but without the total disgrace that would have resulted if he disobeyed orders and refused to make the move. The following day, Roy wrote to his solicitors instructing them not to defend the divorce case:

> *It is my one desire to marry Mrs Buckley – the step I take now I only take for her sake and to avoid otherwise inevitable disgrace. I mean to try and do my best to carry out the instructions of the F[oreign] O[ffice] but if the divorce is thwarted I shall not hesitate to take any step for Mrs Buckley's sake.*

On 24 July, he wrote to Yoï's solicitor, Edward Heron-Allen:

> *I have Sir Charles Hardinge's statement that if I am made a co-respondent I could not remain in the service longer… Nothing will stop me from marrying Yoï when the divorce is granted. It is solely that we should get married – for Yoï is all that I care for in the world – I have fought this Foreign Office business, for so long as a loophole could be found it seemed worth fighting for, and so long as the divorce is certain Yoï need not be long alone. Once again I beg you to do all in your power to get Yoï free so that we can be free and can be married.*

He also wrote a letter of reassurance for Yoï to keep by her:

> *Yoï, I want you to remember whenever things seem difficult and you are unhappy that if you went back to Jim or if ever I knew that you had thought of doing so, it would mean my life.*
>
> *My only desire and intention is that we be married – whatever people say or do, you must always be sure that I am working with that one end in view. For ever and always your Roy.*

On 26 July, he wrote to his mother:

> *I am on my way to Tehran: I am going to do all I can to satisfy the Foreign Office and to avoid dismissal with disgrace – but I want you to realise this as my fixed intention – if the divorce proceedings are stopped I shall not return to Europe alive.*

Yoï now returned to Bad Ems, where she stayed for about five weeks, taking the prescribed cure. Meanwhile, Roy travelled on towards Tehran. This involved a long journey by train to Baku, on the western side of the Caspian Sea, from where a steamer service crossed to the southern shore. The journey then continued overland to Tehran. On 4 August, while waiting for the steamer at Baku, Roy telegraphed Yoï's solicitor:

Can we be sure of divorce shall I proceed?

He received the reply: "Proceed safely".

That same day, in London, the petition for divorce was filed. On 4 September, the British Minister in Tehran, Sir George Barclay, personally served the petition on Roy.

Roy immediately wrote to his solicitors:

I should like a further £100 set aside for Mrs Buckley out of the advance the Kennard trustees have made.

You mention that you propose to enter a formal appearance to the Petition. Do whatever you think best to bring about the divorce as easily for us both as possible and to facilitate our marriage afterwards.

I only want you to bear in mind – these are my sole instructions to you – that Mrs Buckley and I are to be married as soon as possible… Do everything in your power as my representative to make this possible as soon and as easily as possible… You are to act purely and solely on the instructions that I have given you and to lighten matters for Mrs Buckley and for our future.

Early in September, Yoï travelled from Bad Ems to Blankenberge, on the Belgian coast between Ostend and Zeebrugge. She stayed there for about three weeks, taking solitary walks by the sea and making friends with a girl on a nearby farm who taught her how to milk the cows.[53]

The petition for divorce was served on her there. Also during that month, Yoï had a letter from Roy asking if the case could be made more public in the newspapers. His idea was that the publicity would embarrass the Foreign Office and make it anxious to get rid of him. He also asked whether the Court could demand that he should attend at the case, presumably with the same end in view.

At the end of September, Yoï returned to London, probably to consult her solicitor, but by mid-October she was back in Paris. Roy then admitted to her in a letter dated 24 October that when he was in London he had, in fact, agreed to stay in Tehran for at least two years. He continued:

I know there is no chance of Sir Charles Hardinge letting me come back now – that is giving me the permission. They do not believe that the case will come on, and will do everything, put every obstacle in the way to prevent us from meeting and making the divorce proceedings inevitable.

I have at least seen all along that the one thing than can free us from the F. O. and from everyone is the hearing of the case – the proof that we are absolutely determined to get married and to stand the divorce. When they see that it is inevitable they will have no further care or interest in keeping me here – but only the case itself will convince them that it is inevitable. It is for this reason that it is so important for the case to come on and for them all to see that all this time we have been separated has made no difference…

My mother knows exactly my intentions. I have only written to her to repeat the letter I wrote in the train the morning after leaving Nürnberg…

On 26 October, he wrote to Yoï's solicitor:

I have just heard of a threat that my mother is using… It makes me utterly furious to think of the means which are being employed to try and wreck our future… If only Yoï can have strength – But her position is awful… I realise how awful it must be for her.

He did not, however, state what the threat was.

On 27 October, he wired to Yoï:

You know nothing can make any difference.

The next day, in answer to a question from Yoï as to when he would be allowed to come back, he telegraphed:

Fear all depends on case, Yoï, nothing can alter me.

At the beginning of November, Yoï moved to Rome, even though she had no friends or acquaintances there. Roy had asked her to go there and live in his flat. He wrote:

I want you to be there, in our house, amongst the things that I got only for you.

On 6 November, Roy wrote to Yoï to say that he had heard from his grandmother, Lady Kennard, and that Sir Charles Hardinge had been discussing the matter with her. Roy had replied to Lady Kennard:

Mrs Buckley's position has throughout been misrepresented. But I want you to know, and to know directly from me, that it is I who all along compelled every step that has been taken, and taken in the face of bitter opposition.

He also said in his letter to Yoï:

I have just received a kind but firm message from Sir Charles Hardinge, reminding me of the promise I gave the F. O. to stay here until he gives me leave to return. That is all. There is nothing beside that.

I am wondering what it can mean, but it seems very hopeful.

He continued to say that he was very anxious about what Mrs Carew was doing.

In December, Yoï received a worrying letter from Roy:

Every threat, every device is being used and I have only just found out to what depth of vileness people have gone, but I feel perfectly sure that your solicitor and mine will be able to undo them.

I have found out that my mother is only realising now how determined I am to marry you and that the case is really a definite fact…

The important point is this – they have tried every imaginable device on my side, as you yourself knew, but I have reason to believe that they are now trying to bring pressure to bear from your side, and, Yoï, you know already into what forms that pressure may be put. They are quite capable of trying to poison your mind, to prove to you that I went to Tehran to get out of it, to save myself, any lie, and all. Yoï, for God's sake trust no one but our friends.

So few, so few can understand what we know that our life together can be…

I realise what you are suffering, what every bit of it must be, but remember that it is to their interest to try to make your position impossible, and again I repeat I should not now be surprised at any means they employed. I know that at the present moment my mother is using every means to avert the case, but as long as you remain firm and there is no doubt in your mind, as there can be none in mine, that nothing in the world shall be allowed to keep us apart, so long as that… we shall triumph.

… if once I was at home, I don't know what my mother, in the mad state she is in, might not do.

I have felt all along that when the case is heard we shall be free, but only then in reality… It is imperative that the case should come on, and come on quickly, and with the gaining of our liberty all this will be ended too…

For once my mother sees that it is inevitable, sees, I suppose, that I am a co-respondent, all this will cease… But don't let them harass you, don't listen to people who come and make things appear so black, and listen only to those who have really charge of the affair, and to our love… try to realise that the case is the goal with our life beyond.

On 5 December, he wrote:

Now at last I do realise what suffering your life must be at Rome. All along I had hoped to find an easy way to return to you and avoid the horror which I realise that the mere fact of the dismissal would bring on those for whom I once cared. From what I now hear from the F. O. I know they intend to demand from me the full period of my time here, but that is not all. They tell me that the divorce will make no difference to my position in the Diplomatic Service… This I heard directly to-day.

Little one, all along I have known that my life however it may be, must be yours always – We are and always shall remain one… Whatever the F. O. say or do, nothing will ever alter that, nor my desire and intention that we should be married at last and live together…

You could not think that all we have passed through together, all that we have gained together, could be anything but for our whole lives together, nor that I could ever change.

But I am so utterly in despair, and I cannot, cannot bear to know all that you are suffering there, and that I am so inadequate.

I have everything that belongs to you around me. Little one, I love you – that is stronger and more than all.

In answer to a letter of Yoï's in which she had said that even if he changed, he must know that he could tell her so, that he must know she was his friend beyond everything else, he wrote:

Why do you write such things, you know what you are for me, why I am here. Every day that goes by is something conquered for your sake. I know what your days must be. I want you to tell me if you feel you cannot bear any more, tell me as you would if we were together, not weighing all kinds of considerations, just tell me all, and I will come to you in face of everything. I am only living for you to be my wife.

In her reply, Yoï suggested that he should speak to Sir George Barclay, telling him everything. Not surprisingly, Roy replied that he could not discuss the subject with him – that Sir George Barclay could not understand such things.

Roy wrote to his solicitor and on 18 December told Yoï he had done so to 'enforce my instructions.'

At the beginning of January 1910, Roy was still writing affectionately to Yoï. However, it later emerged that his behaviour at this time was not as open and straightforward as he led her to believe. In that same month, he wrote to his solicitors giving instructions for the removal of his furniture from the flat in Rome at the end of his tenancy on 1 May. He did not tell Yoï of this, even though he knew she was now living there. Meanwhile, back in London, Roy's mother and her friends were claiming that he had already agreed to give up Yoï altogether.

Yoï and her solicitor were expecting her divorce case to be scheduled for hearing soon after the law courts reopened after the Christmas break. But on 15 January, a telegram from friends in London told her that Roy was now going to defend the case. His solicitors succeeded in getting the hearing postponed to give them more time to prepare. Yoï by this time was quite ill from the anxiety of not knowing what was really happening but, nevertheless, was still totally convinced that Roy would stand by her and that he was acting under duress from his mother and her friends. She told her solicitor:

Believe in Roy whatever you do. Remember, I say he has been trapped. No one on earth can shake my belief in him and I know I am right.

Then on 27 January, she received a telegram suggesting she should think seriously about going back to her husband:

My position has been made such with regard to case that I am forced to beg you to consider possibility of return
Royoï

As this was signed by their two names combined, which they had previously agreed would mean that everything between them was all right, she took this to mean that the Foreign Office were forcing him to do something against his will, or that some unforeseen legal problem had arisen. But only a few days later, various friends of Roy's told Yoï's friends in London that they had received letters from him stating that his feelings had changed and that he now had no intention of marrying her.

On 7 February 1910, the divorce case finally came on for hearing. Roy had changed his mind yet again and offered no defence. A decree nisi was pronounced and the custody of the children given to James Buckley. The following day *The Times* gave the following account:

MR. BARNARD, K.C. (with whom was Mr. Bayford), said that the parties were married at Trinity Church, Paddington, on April 21, 1896, and had lived together at Castell Gorfod, St. Clears, Carmarthenshire, and in London, and there were two children issue of the marriage. They lived fairly happily together until the early part of 1909. In December, 1908, or the beginning of January, 1909, the petitioner met the co-respondent, who was visiting at his house at Norfolk-square, when the respondent introduced him. He saw him three times, and he objected to the acquaintance that had been formed between his wife and the co-respondent. In May 1909, the petitioner and his family were returning to Wales, but the respondent said that she wished to stay with a lady friend in Paris, and the petitioner consented to her going. In June the petitioner came to London from Wales; he returned after a short absence, and on June 23 there was handed to him a letter from the respondent dated June 16. The letter was as follows: "I have gone away with Coleridge Kennard. When you are angry and bitter remember I have left my children and everything." The petitioner endeavoured to ascertain where his wife was, but without success. On July 23, however, he received a letter from the co-respondent, conceived in the following terms:

"Dear Captain Buckley, – I am writing to ask you if you would be so good as to let me be served with a writ for divorce as soon as possible. I had hoped to have been served with it, personally, before leaving England, but the conditions imposed by the Foreign Office, with which I feel it right to conform for Yoï's sake and our future, compel me to leave England to-morrow. I have ascertained with regret that the matter is not far enough advanced for the step to be taken before then… My solicitors have my instructions to facilitate in every way the serving of the writ and the granting of the divorce. We fear that there are a great many people working against Yoï. Truly yours, COLERIDGE KENNARD."

Evidence having been given that the respondent and co-respondent had stayed together at the Hotel Russell from July 11 to July 16, 1909, the learned PRESIDENT pronounced a decree nisi, with costs, and gave the petitioner custody of the children.[54]

That same day, Yoï's solicitor, Edward Heron-Allen, wrote to Roy Kennard in an attempt to clarify the situation:

My dear Roy,

You must have come to the conclusion that I am a most appallingly bad correspondent and it is an accusation of which I admit the justice, but really ever since the beginning of November I have been so busy that excepting in case of absolute necessity it has been impossible for me to write letters.

The case of absolute necessity has now arisen.

The decree nisi in Yoï's case was pronounced today, as you will no doubt hear by this mail and it becomes necessary for me, as the only person officially looking after her, to know exactly how she stands.

For some time past everybody has been telling Yoï and me that you are tired of the situation and have determined to abandon her to her fate. I do not believe that there is one shadow of truth in this; not only having regard to the ethical impossibility of any man behaving in such a way to a woman whom he ever even pretended to care for, but also having regard to what we know of you and your own letters, especially one which is before me, in which you even warn her that every threat and device will be used to shake her faith in you, and in which you say "They are quite capable of trying to poison your mind and prove to you that I went to Tehran to get out of it and save myself ."

The day before yesterday I had a long interview – with Ross – in which he told me categorically that you had changed your mind. He had been to see me the day before, on which occasion he told me that he had received letters from you for some weeks past, and that Holman had done the same, and that in all these letters you express yourself as having come to your senses and being tired of the situation. I replied that I would not believe it unless you telegraphed me using the code word (by which you signed a recent important telegram) corroborating what he said.

On Saturday he produced a telegram purporting to come from you which read as follows: "Feelings have changed find it impossible to marry her or continue present relations have no code to Allen so I do not repeat. Roy".

I took upon myself to believe that this telegram was a forgery. The main burden of his desire was that the petition should be withdrawn, a course which would have left Yoï stranded and alone, without even you to protect her and would have left Buckley to pay the whole of the costs. I repeat that I agree with Yoï in trusting you implicitly and in believing everything that you have said in your letters to her, but the time has come when I must tell you what is being done and said in your name, and must have your explicit repudiation of the things they have tried to saddle upon you.

If by any horrible chance there should be any truth in what they say, I ask you as man to man to write and tell me that you have changed your mind and intend to leave Yoï to face the fate which you have forced on her. Nothing short of this under your own hand will ever shatter her belief in you. If I receive this it will become my duty to go to see her to see what could be done towards righting what you have done. Please write immediately on receipt of this.

No reply was ever received to this letter. Yoï herself felt unable to believe anything that Robert Ross had said as Roy had explicitly warned her not to trust him while they were still together in London. She told her solicitor in a letter dated 21 February that until she heard from Roy himself, face-to-face, that his feelings had changed, she would not believe it. Only a week later, she was told that Roy's solicitors in London had heard from him, saying:

It is my uninfluenced determination to sever all connection with her if possible.

Yoï had by now been on her own in Rome for nearly four months, but she still could not believe that Roy's feelings towards her had changed so dramatically. She was completely convinced that he was acting under pressure from his mother. And so, on 2 March 1910, confused and unhappy, but determined to confront him in person, she left Rome and set out for Tehran.

To Tehran and Back

The land journey from Rome to Tehran would be daunting enough to a modern traveller, but in 1910 it must have been an immense undertaking. Yoï travelled by train from Rome to Vienna and then boarded another train that took her across Austria, Hungary and part of Russia to Baku, on the west coast of the Caspian Sea. From here, she would take the steamer south to Persia. Overall, the journey was to last fourteen days.

We cannot be sure of her exact route between Vienna and Baku, but the most likely would seem to be from Vienna to Budapest, then via Bucharest, Odessa, and Petrovsk to Baku. This part of the journey lasted five days, during which she met and befriended a young woman who was returning from England to her family home in the Caucasus.

> *I met her in the train when travelling between Vienna and Baku; for five days we sat facing each other. We tried to read, it was not easy; we tried to look out of the window, the steadily falling sleet prevented us from seeing anything, but we could feel that outside lay the pitiless undulating steppes.* [55]

The two young women passed the time in lengthy discussions about the nature of love and human relationships – they both had left their husbands, so they had much in common. Later, Yoï would write:

> *Five days in a Russian train may be in friendship like five years in a great city.* [56]

Finally, the train reached Baku, where oil had been discovered some sixty years earlier. The oil fields had been developed over that period and were now the largest in the world, with over 2000 wells producing oil on an industrial scale, and very many smaller ones. Yoï had heard descriptions of the area from other travellers:

People had always described Baku in such a lurid manner to me that I vaguely imagined a town with houses floating on canals of oil, where if one struck a match one ran the risk of starting a fire which would last for years. I imagined that the smell of naphtha was overpowering, and that the Caspian was a sea of oil, so when nearing it in the train I expected to enter the fifth chasm of the Inferno. However, instead of finding anything horrible or beautiful, we arrived at a railway station very much like any other, but that it had something of the appearance of the Alhambra in London, and on the steps leading to it were standing and lying many men belonging to almost every race under the sun.[57]

A "dapper little Frenchman" offered her his services as an interpreter and soon Yoï was climbing into a small open carriage with two strong young horses and a Russian driver.

At last we stopped in front of an insignificant-looking house and went in to find – as if it were the first surprise of the East – a large place with a courtyard in which trees were growing. The hotel was filled with men; very few women travel in that part of the world, and all the men were travelling on business. Traders going to Bokhara and Samarkand, merchants of the Eastern Trading Company, silkworm dealers, Armenians, Tartars, people of all kinds, and all apparently busy discussing affairs or writing in the large room which was used as reading-room, bar and sitting-room.[58]

The next part of her journey would involve a steamer from Baku southwards to the Persian coast. However, the ship was delayed by a gale, so the next day Yoï made herself comfortable with a book in the hotel bar and waited for the weather to improve. There she heard two men speaking Hungarian, the language of her childhood. She spoke to the older man:

"It is good in such a strange place to hear that language." He rose as I spoke and came to where I sat – he looked proud and dignified, a Hungarian of the truest type;

he bowed and presented himself, telling me his name. He then sat down and we
talked about Hungary: he told me where he lived, I told him of the place where I
was born; he had known people I cared for, I knew the mountain castle which was
his home. He was on his way to see some forests on the other side of the Caspian, I
was on my way to Persia; we were both stopped by the gale from being able to cross
– no ships could leave the harbour.[59]

Even though she was later to describe the population of Baku as wilder
and rougher than almost anywhere else in the world, Yoï had earlier been
out to explore the bazaars on the hill in the town. She had also wandered
around the European shops, which were filled with:

… expensive and abominable things – extremely high-heeled boots with garish
leather tops, gramophones in cases on which were painted naked women, over-
ornamented German silver, jewellery twisted into every kind of unpleasant form
– all the horrors that are ousting the things which come from the East.[60]

She had also seen men lying drunk on the pavements, women whom she
described as looking hunted, and even witnessed a fight in which knives
were drawn. Her new acquaintance was horrified to hear that she had
been walking about on her own. He asked if he could take her to see the
oil fields and she eagerly agreed. They found a carriage and driver, and
set off. On their way, Yoï was impressed by the variety and colour of the
clothing of people walking on the promenade. There was anything from
the latest Paris styles to Cossack uniforms. She was also very impressed
with the oil fields:

Leaning against a wall trying to get shelter from the wind, we stood looking at the
vivid colour of everything in the sun, at the black towers standing against the green
sea, at the utter desolation of the surrounding land, half stupefied with astonishment
at the monstrous beauty of all we saw.[61]

That evening, she dined with the old Hungarian. He told her of his life
and children, now all grown up, so he was alone, for his wife had died
young and he missed her still. They talked too of journeys they had
made and of the strong desire to travel that they both shared. Finally,

the old man asked her if she would agree to be his adopted grandchild, as they were both alone in the world. He suggested that they would be able to travel together to see all the things that she cared for and had spoken of.

But then the French interpreter arrived to tell her that the gale had died away and that the ship would be leaving in a few hours. Yoï thanked her elderly friend but told him she would prefer to be alone – always. He came to the ship to see her off and stood on the quayside watching her until it sailed.

The steamer took her to the port of Anzali, in Persia, which is now part of Bandar-e Anzali, in modern Iran. From here, she had an overland journey of some 270 km to reach Tehran, over unmade roads and passing caravans of camels laden with goods. On 16 March, she finally reached Tehran and booked into the hotel there. It had been fourteen days since she left Rome.

Later that day, she called at Roy Kennard's house. He was at dinner but sent word to say he was out. Yoï later found out that he had immediately gone to the Legation to see Sir George and Lady Barclay. He had then asked for, and obtained from Sir George Barclay, leave of absence from Tehran.

Yoï was now handed a note ordering her to leave the house immediately. A Mr Knox of the Consular Service came to make sure that she carried out this instruction. Instead, she complained to him about the terms in which the note was written, suggesting that a communication in such terms could not be intended for her. He at once recognised that he had to apologise for sending it – presumably he had been instructed to see that she left and had not realised he was dealing with an English lady. Yoï now left a note for Roy, who replied saying he would not see her.

The following day, Roy left Tehran and went shooting. Lady Barclay, accompanied by a Mr Lancelot Oliphant, a third secretary in the Legation, called on Yoï to tell her that Roy Kennard was not going to see her and told her to leave Tehran at once. The two of them called on Yoï again the following day, and then for a third time the day after that. In the course of the rather strained conversations that took place, Lady Barclay repeated that Roy would not see Yoï; in fact, he never wanted to see her again, as he was a young man who knew "on which side his bread was buttered". When Yoï asked Lady Barclay what right she had to interfere in her personal affairs she replied that she came as a friend of Sir Coleridge Kennard. Yoï told her she could not believe this, as in many of his letters Roy had expressed his dislike of Lady Barclay.

One evening, when Yoï had felt unwell and had retired to bed, they called on her again and insisted on seeing her. They stayed from 10.30 pm until midnight, arguing with her and attempting to get her to sign a paper agreeing to leave Tehran on a set date if she was allowed to see him. This she refused to do, dismissing it as an extreme impertinence. Lady Barclay did go so far as to say that if the divorce did succeed then she would revise her opinion of Roy Kennard and would consider him a blackguard. However, she thought this was impossible. The next day, Yoï received a terse note from Roy:

> *As I hear you will not leave Tehran without a personal interview am prepared to grant one tomorrow. C. Kennard*

He insisted that he should bring a witness and suggested that she bring a witness too, but as she knew no one in Tehran, Mr Oliphant agreed to act as witness for both of them.

The interview took place the following day, Thursday 24 March. Yoï began by explaining that she had come to Tehran specifically because Roy had previously warned her not to trust anyone, and not to believe anything negative that was written as if it came from him. But Roy did not let her finish. He interrupted her, claiming that she knew very well why he had changed, repeating 'You know – you know' and 'I hate you.' Yoï begged him to explain, but he would say nothing more and left the room. She rushed after him and, catching hold of him, again begged him to explain. Finally, he told her that his mother had put into his hands proofs of collusion, and went on to say:

> *I am taking action against you for collusion. We are now plaintiff and defendant, and enemies. I will not tell you anything – it might injure my case.*

Collusion – agreement between husband and wife to attempt to obtain a divorce – was very much frowned upon at the time, and if it were proved it would have certainly resulted in the case being thrown out, with Roy being seen as the injured party.

Yoï then went to see Sir George Barclay and asked him to help her to get a more detailed explanation from Roy – one that she could understand. Rather ironically, after the way his wife had been behaving, Sir George said he could not intervene in their private affairs. She then wrote to Sir George, asking him to read this letter to Roy, and went on to protest her innocence:

> *I say that what he believes is untrue – that those proofs were either forged or of false witness, and were used before the divorce as a desperate means to stop the case. He must now do as he said and bring an action against me, so that I can prove I am absolutely innocent.*

Sir George never replied to this letter and there was no further communication from Roy either. Yoï at last had to admit to herself that the situation was hopeless.

In the hotel, she had been surrounded by men, all talking about their business affairs. The only person who had spoken to her was an Irishman. She found him to be extremely knowledgeable about Persian life, the city, the tales and legends, and the countryside around Tehran. Each evening, she dined with him and three of his friends. They went for walks to see the bazaars, the small squares with their fountains, and to admire the views of the distant mountains. She found consolation in the beauty of the surrounding countryside and shared something of her feelings with him, telling him:

> *Fate has taken from me everything that a human being can lose, and I can still say 'Joy is mine', because I see the mountains around us are blue, the shadows in their valleys purple; from the trees in the enclosed garden at our feet the wind blows towards us a shower of rose-pink blossoms; the grass is a fresh spring green, the desert is gold-dust and endless as are our thoughts; the little stream sings all the time in the sun; and when the night comes I love the stars, and the snow on the mountain-tops that in their light shines white against the sky, and I think that I can say this because I am no longer myself, but by suffering have become part of all those things.* [62]

After a few more days in Tehran, she started early one sunny morning on the long journey back to Rome – the only home she now had. As she left, she looked back to Mount Damávand, the highest peak in Persia, with a special place in the Persian mythology and folklore. She travelled in a coach with four horses, even taking the reins herself at times. The driver was young – they tried to communicate but could find no common language. By the time they reached the post-house where the horses and driver were to be changed, the sky had darkened and a storm appeared imminent. The road ahead climbed into the mountains, and as they set out with a new team of horses, the storm burst. Late that night, after hours of travelling through the wind and rain, they reached the next post-house, but as all the rooms were full, with people even sleeping on the floor, she persuaded the driver to go on.

For four more hours they drove through the darkness and reached the next post-house. Again, all the rooms were full, but one man woke and put down a carpet on the floor and then brought her a brazier of burning charcoal. Yoï lay down, covered herself with a fur coat, and slept. When she woke, she found a Cossack kneeling on the floor looking curiously at her.

Someone now told her that the road she had just travelled over was now blocked by falling rocks brought down by the storm, and that it would be days before it would be open again. If they had stopped at the first post-house, they would have been trapped. But the road was clear in the opposite direction, towards Rasht. For hours, they drove alongside the swollen river, passing caravans of camels heading towards Tehran with goods from the port. At Rasht, Yoï booked into the same hotel that she had stayed at on her outward journey to Tehran and was delighted to find that the owner's dog, a large white Pomeranian called Matros, seemed to remember her. Yoï later was to write of this meeting:

> *He jumped on to the sofa, on to the chairs, on to my boxes, on to the bed; he couldn't keep still, he was so pleased, and I was so glad that someone was pleased to see me that I sat down by him on the floor, put my head on his coat, and cried.*[63]

In the bar that evening, she found a Russian merchant who told her, in German, that he had telegraphed to the port at Anzali and that the steamer from Baku had not been able to land because of the storm. No boat of any kind was leaving for two days, so she made up her mind to be patient and to see something of Rasht. The next day, with Matros accompanying her, she explored the bazaars and shops in the town. Later, they walked a short distance out into the country towards the rice fields, where they sat on a rock and watched flocks of snipe and teal, as well as the occasional heron and bittern, and to her delight, found ponds filled with wild tortoises.

The next day, Yoï left Rasht on the road towards Anzali. The dog seemed determined to come with her, jumping into the carriage and twice having to be removed by his owner. At the port, she boarded the boat for Baku and, after many more days and nights of travelling, she finally reached Rome on Monday 18 April. Her journey to Tehran and back had lasted nearly seven weeks.

Yoï took over the lease of the Rome flat in the *Trinità dei Monti* in her own name from 1 May. That same day, the contractors arrived to remove all the contents. In spite of Roy Kennard's letter the previous November, in which he had said that he wanted to think of Yoï in their flat, amongst the things he had bought especially for her, only two months later he had instructed his solicitors to arrange the removal of all the furniture when the lease expired. Roy celebrated his 25th birthday on 12 May. The Kennard inheritance was now his to spend as he saw fit, free from the control of the trustees.

After the stress of the previous few months, Yoï again became ill. During the months of June, July and August, she rested and recovered high in the hills to the east of Rome, spending some time at the hill village of Bellegra, and later at a convent at Subiaco. Her room in the convent had frescos on both walls and ceilings, with windows looking out to a fountain and a cherry tree. She took gentle strolls around the convent, or sat quietly reading or gazing into the distance, and tried to make sense of what had happened to her.

Meanwhile, in London, on 24 August, the decree nisi was made absolute. In spite of Roy's threats, no attempt to block this on grounds of collusion was ever made.

Other London news and opinion would have reached her from her great-aunt, Theresa Berkeley, who had always been close to Yoï. The news from London was not good – Mrs Carew and her friends were still maintaining that they had proof of collusion. Yoï felt that it was essential to clear her name, if not for her own sake then for her children. In October, she wrote once more, and at some length, to Sir George Barclay, pleading with him to persuade Roy Kennard and Lady Barclay to withdraw the allegations they had made against her. However, Sir George again did not reply to her letter. Instead, he recommended that Roy should be promoted and on 30 November it was reported in the *London Gazette* that the King had appointed Sir Coleridge Arthur Fitzroy Kennard to be a Third Secretary.[64]

On 5 November, in a last attempt to get help, Yoï wrote to Mr Oliphant in Tehran, asking him to approach Roy Kennard on her behalf. She received the following reply:

> *Madam*
> *I have to acknowledge receipt of your letter of 15th ultimo.*
> *I regret to have to reply that I consider my position must prevent my asking Sir C. Kennard any question on your behalf, as it would likewise prevent my transmitting to you any question on his behalf.*
> *Pray believe me yours truly*
> *Lancelot Oliphant*

She had no other witness to the meeting in Tehran and no one else to turn to for help. In addition, in spite of the divorce having been made absolute and Roy Kennard having maintained a complete silence, Yoï heard that Lady Barclay was continuing to speak against her and was becoming even more friendly with Roy. This information was confirmed when on 5 January 1911, *The Times* and *Morning Post* announced that:

> *A marriage has been arranged and will take place shortly between Sir Arthur Fitzroy Coleridge Kennard, attaché to H. B. M. Legation at Tehran, and Dorothy, daughter of Sir George Barclay, British Minister to Persia, and Lady Barclay.*[65]

Roy Kennard duly married Dorothy Barclay at the British Legation in Tehran on 5 April 1911.[66] Only four years later, he left her for an actress, and Dorothy divorced him on the grounds of his desertion and adultery in 1918.[67]

Italy

Now alone in Rome, and feeling unable to return to England due to the scandal of the divorce and Roy Kennard's treatment of her, Yoï accepted her situation and attempted to get on with her life. She began to write down some of her memories of her travels. She gradually got to know Rome, walking for miles around its streets. She made new friends, mixing with local musicians, artists and students and sometimes going with them to concert rehearsals. Among them was the pianist Carlo Angelelli. But above all she enjoyed the company of an attractive young sculptor whose full name was Antonio Nicola Giovanni Enrico Mario Maraini. In 1911, the year in which they first met, Antonio was just twenty-five, nine years younger than Yoï herself.

While Antonio was growing up, many intellectuals, painters, sculptors and musicians used to visit the Marainis' house in Rome where his father, Enrico, would offer them help and support. Enrico had expected his son to become a lawyer, but Antonio gradually became more and more convinced that he was to be some sort of artist, although initially he did not know if he would become a painter, a sculptor or a man of letters. Gradually, once his law studies were behind him, he had turned more and more to sculpture.

In 1911, Yoï's first book, entitled *A Year of Strangers*, was published in London. She used the pen-name Yoï Pawlowska, and dedicated the book to her two children, Wilma and Gabriel Ifor (Gabor) Buckley. The book contains impressions of many of the people and places she met on her journey to Tehran and back. She included a short introduction:

I have just finished a year of my life, during which I have seen only strangers and no one whom I had known before. These are some of the strangers who have become my friends.

Though I have headed each sketch by the name of one of them, I do not, of course, mean these pages to be in any way an account of their lives or personalities, but only an impression of a few of the moments which we have passed together.[68]

The final chapter in the book is about Antonio, whom she calls "the Faun". He comes across as a young man who is bounding with energy and enthusiasm for life and all it has to offer. Poetry, architecture, literature:

... he is nearly always smiling; he is a Roman and a sculptor, and he has a name, though no one can call him anything but Faun. He carries with him everywhere the gaiety of forest life, the haunting shade of leafy valleys, the laughter of running water, the little cries of surprised wild things, the joy of wood flowers and the glancing of sunlight on green moss through trembling branches.

It is difficult to believe he has a home just as other people have, and that he lives with human beings who are dear to him. When he runs down the many flights of marble steps I expect him to disappear into the mountains or into the old ilex wood near Villa Medici, or even into that dark temple on the Palatine into which a small waterfall drops noisily and ceaselessly. But I know it is quite different. He often speaks of his home and his relations, and from what he says I think of them all as a pack of happy children dancing on green lawns and always laughing in the sun.[69]

Almost immediately, Yoï became Antonio's favourite model. The frontispiece of *A Year of Strangers* is an engraving based on his sculpture entitled *Yoï con l'idolo egizio (Yoï with the Egyptian idol)*. It is a full-length representation of Yoï holding a statuette.

By early 1912, Yoï was pregnant. About this time, she got to know Mary Berenson, who was visiting Rome with her husband, the American art collector and connoisseur Bernard Berenson. He was widely regarded as the pre-eminent authority on Renaissance art.[70] Mary, *née* Smith, was a notable art historian in her own right. She was the sister of Logan Pearsall Smith and of Alys Pearsall Smith, the first wife of Bertrand Russell. The Berensons had a home near Florence at the villa *I Tatti*, which they had bought in 1905, and in 1909 they had commissioned two

young Englishmen, Cecil Ross Pinsent and Geoffrey Scott, to redesign
the garden. Scott was Bernard Berenson's secretary at the time.

When Mary discovered that Yoï was pregnant, she became very
protective of her, encouraging her to move to Florence where she could
give her some support. Antonio's family was objecting strongly to any
thought he might have of marrying Yoï – his mother was strongly Roman
Catholic and could not contemplate her son marrying a divorcée, let alone
one who was a foreigner and nine years older than he was.

At last, supported and encouraged by Yoï, and perhaps influenced
by the Berensons, Antonio made the decision to devote his life fully to
art. Early in 1912, he bought a farm at Ricorboli, to the south-east of
Florence, a city he had loved and idealised since the years of his youth.[71]
Their new home was at *99 Via Ponte a Ema*, although the address later
became *99 Via Benedetto Fortini,* when the road was renamed in 1918.
The farm was worked on the sharecropping system known in Italy as
mezzadria, in which the landowner allows a tenant to use the land and
provides housing and equipment in return for a half-share of the crop
produced on the land.

Later that year, on 15 November 1912, Yoï gave birth to a son. They
named him Fosco.

At some time in 1912, in an attempt to clear her name, Yoï had taken
the unusual step of writing and publishing a full account of her affair
with Roy Kennard. A copy of this thirty-four-page booklet survives in
the British Library, with handwritten corrections and additions by her
solicitor, Edward Heron-Allen. In her introduction, Yoï says:

*Owing to the fact that Sir Coleridge Kennard's friends are giving many reasons,
not any of them true ones, as to why he has behaved to me in the way in which he
has, I have been forced to write out a statement showing how untrue are the things
that they have said all through.*

*I have written to him since our interview in Tehran, saying that if he will
only write and tell me that he has done all merely because of change in his feelings
towards me, I could forgive him everything and we could part as friends; and that
all I ask is that he should write to some of those of his mother's friends who have
been persistently spreading gross calumnies about me, telling them the true facts.
He has not answered me. I have written two or three times to Sir George Barclay*

asking him to get some explanation of Sir Coleridge Kennard and to try to get some semblance of justice for me: he has said that he could do nothing.

I mention these things to show that I have tried in every possible way to save any further discussion about this affair and if Sir Coleridge Kennard had written to those friends of his, as I asked him to, the matter would have ended. Those friends still continue to speak against me, and it has been made clear to me that because of this I must not let the matter drop.

Sir Coleridge Kennard and his friends know that because of the position in which he has placed me I am unable to return to England, and owing to that am not able to see friends who could help me to get justice. He and they have everything in their favour, but I hope that these facts will speak for me.

E. C. Buckley.

I have set out in the following pages a clear statement of the position in which I have been placed, because I feel that the facts have not been known, and that thus many things that have been alleged against me may have gained credence.

I am sure few people can have understood how I was treated in Tehran – how Lady Barclay and her friends heaped every kind of insult upon me and did their utmost to prevent my seeing Sir Coleridge Kennard, and how everyone combined to protect and encourage him in his refusal to give any word of explanation at all, except the one accusation of collusion between my husband and myself, which he knew was untrue.

The marriage which has since been announced between Sir Coleridge Kennard and Lady Barclay's daughter may possibly seem to some people a kind of proof that this treatment of me was justified. That is why I want now to set all the facts out fully and clearly; and I know that anyone who learns the truth will say that it was utterly unjustifiable.

As to his refusal to marry me, after he had made me be divorced and lose my children and everything for him, I can say nothing. The last letter he wrote to me was similar in tone to all the others from the first. Then silence. I went to Tehran alone when I could bear it no longer. I had to stand alone fighting against everyone there in the British Legation before I was granted an interview. At that interview I was told nothing, and ever since have met with absolute silence.

Mrs Carew, I know, has told people that it was I who urged Sir Coleridge Kennard to go away, and that I tried to "plunder him of his fortune" and that I had a great deal of money from him; that the money settled as a marriage settlement was given me to end everything and set him free and finally that there had been collusion between my husband and myself about the divorce and Lady Barclay has herself said that she has spread these things.

People have not known the facts. I want them to know them and judge for themselves whether these things are true – to set things out quite clearly and in such a form that anyone may be able to verify them, the only way was to give the actual words spoken and written, so I have done this.[72]

It is not known how many copies were circulated, or what effect it had in London society, but as Edward Heron-Allen gave his approval to its printing it seems likely that he was making protests on her behalf. Certainly, within a year or so Yoï again felt able to visit England.

Late in 1912, her second book, *Those that Dream*, was published. Reviewing it in the literary supplement to the monthly arts magazine *Rhythm*, Filson Young compares it with her earlier work:

"A Year of Strangers" was a collection of sketches of people and things in Italy and the Far East; it was the harvest of a year of solitary wanderings on the part of one at whom life had dealt a blow, and whose own heart had driven her out into the wilderness to re-discover and possess again her own soul. And although this is not the book which I am discussing at present, I would like to take this opportunity of advising everyone who has not read it to read and keep "A Year of Strangers." That was Yoï Pawlowska's first book; "Those that Dream" is her second, more ambitious in design, less successful in achievement, but no less interesting as an expression of the mind of the writer.

It is a picture rather than a story, a picture of the lives of two or three highly civilised women, and of the country about Rome and the Sabine hills. There are also little scenes in the lives of artists, little miniatures of peasant life; but there is no story in any real sense of the word. The figures and characters in the book are mere excuses for the author to express her own mind about things; but we need not object to that, for it is really her own mind, her own thoughts, her own vision, which we wish to share. Her characteristics are a most sensitive love of beauty, an affinity with beautiful things, and a clear and patient perception of them, combined with an unusual strength of mind – a sense of fairness which is not really a common attribute of the feminine intelligence. Injustice and cruelty are her two unforgivable sins; and ugliness is almost unforgivable. Consequently her outlook upon life is a large and simple one, which embraces every kind of waywardness if it be the result of a genuine curiosity about life, or a whole-hearted search after joy and beauty; but injustice and cruelty, wherever they are encountered in the tangled affairs of mankind, seem to loom before her mind like gigantic rocks that cast a shadow in which the soul suddenly shivers and grows afraid.

What one may clumsily describe as a deep spiritual sensuality is characteristic of this book and its writing; a fear of the shadow of the two rocks, a desire to keep running back into the sun, and (by whatever other name it may be disguised) to continue the search for joy. Delightful and melancholy are the cadences in which Yoï Pawlowska often clothes her thoughts, but the melancholy is a thin disguise. "It is good to be loved," she says; "it is better to love: but best of all to stand alone with the wind in your face, the endless plain in front of you, the burning sun over your head… and in your soul a hope that you have kept faith with yourself." Such a sentence is rarely written except by someone who has done all these things, and fully enjoyed doing them. To a nature like this, even pain and suffering are a kind of delight; for they are sensations, and in sensations, cutting or caressing, sharp or sweet, such a nature must find its life…[73]

The magazine *Rhythm* in which this review appeared was edited by John Middleton Murry and Katherine Mansfield. A literary, arts, and critical review magazine, it was published in London from 1911 to 1913. Yoï herself contributed to the February 1913 edition. Her article entitled *In the Campagna* is a collection of somewhat enigmatic short items, mostly one or two sentences long. Here are just a few of them:

If you asked the stream why it sang, it would answer: "The cruel stones cut me as knives cut, and I sing so that I shall not cry."
The little bird drank from the trough of the black pig. She is still a bird.
When the wild flowers are round us and the air smells of mint and of the sea, we hold each other's hands. But in the market place you stand with the men, and I cannot listen to the gossip of the women.
If the round world were an eye, how far could it see into Eternity?
The night falls on the earth; it creeps into the crevasses of the ice and lies on the fire at the bottom of a crater.[74]

Yoï was still part of Mary Berenson's circle of friends, and for a time Geoffrey Scott seems to have been fascinated by her, to the point of believing himself in love with her and that she felt the same for him. Certainly, Mary and Geoffrey both seemed to feel that Yoï and Antonio were fundamentally unsuited to each other. But early in 1914, Yoï and Antonio visited London, and it was there, on 26 March, that they were married, by licence, at the register office in the district of St Martin. One of their witnesses was Ernest Daintrey, a Streatham solicitor; the other was their old friend the pianist Carlo Angelelli, whom they had known in Rome. A few weeks later, he would make his London debut at the Steinway Hall.[75]

In June 1914, Yoï's third book was published. *A Child Went Forth* was a slightly fictionalised account of her childhood in Tállya. The dedication reads simply: "To Theresa Berkeley", in a gesture of gratitude for the care and affection she had received over the years from her great-aunt.

In *Punch,* the anonymous reviewer greeted the new book with enthusiasm:

> *The name of Madame Yoï Pawlowska is new to me; but if her previous books were anything like so good as* A Child Went Forth *(Duckworth) I am heartily sorry to have missed them. There have been many books written about childhood, and the end of them is not yet in sight; but I have known none that so successfully attains the simplicity that should belong to the subject. You probably identify the title as a quotation from Walt Whitman, about the child that went forth every day, "and the first object that he looked upon, that object he became."*
>
> *The child in the present instance was one Anna, who went forth in the Hungarian village where she was born, and saw and became a number of picturesque and amusing things, all of which her narrator has quite obviously herself recalled, and set down in excellent fashion. I don't want you to run away with the idea that Anna was a good or even a pleasant child. Anything but that. The things she did and said furnished a more than sufficient reason for her father to threaten again and again to send her to school in England. The book ends with the realisation of this, which had always been to Anna as a kind of shadowy horror in the background of life. We are not told which particular English school was favoured with her patronage, nor how she got on there. I was too interested in her career not to be sorry for this omission; and that shall be my personal tribute to her attractions.*[76]

About this time, while on holiday by the sea, Yoï became friendly with the great Italian actress Eleonora Duse. She later described their meeting:

It was at Viareggio, at a moment when the place was almost deserted, that I first met Eleonora Duse. She spent many hours on the shore looking at the sea, and as she had been ill, fearing to disturb her, I did not go near to where she sat. But when she saw me playing with a baby on the sands she waved a white scarf, and as the wind blew it towards us, she called out, "Come, come." It was easy to see why convalescence was, for her, a difficult and lengthy business; she always gave too much of herself to all with whom she came in contact; when the baby rolled on the sands she leant forward from her chair encouraging him, playing at the same time a little pantomime in the air with her hands, to make him laugh.[77]

They found they both knew the dancer Isadora Duncan, who had recently lost both her children in a tragic accident in Paris. Later, Eleonora moved to Florence and often visited Yoï. In September 1915, Yoï and Antonio's second son Harry was born, but just a year later, he died. At the time, Eleonora was in Sardinia, making her only film, *Cenere (Ashes)*. Yoï later wrote:

There was a moment when she was away acting, for the first time, for the cinematograph. When she heard that a disastrous epidemic had also left us mourning, as soon as she returned she came to see me. Even the sight of her and the knowledge of the courage with which, in spite of her immense capacity for suffering – equal only to her capacity for delight – she had faced every difficulty, could not rouse me. At once, seeing this, she started trying to interest me; she, who never talks of herself, began to tell me of her adventures when acting for the film. She was soon absorbed in every detail. "Will it one day be something wonderful – a really new art?" And again "Look – this is how I moved." She then acted for me her part in 'Ashes.' At last, when she sat down, I put my head on her knees; she pushed back the hair from my eyes and made me look up. "Courage, Courage. We must face everything with courage." Then – with her smile that is a flash of hope – "Or how could we go on at all?"[78]

War had broken out in Europe in June 1914, although Italy took no part in it until the following year. As a result, Antonio was away from home for long periods, for at least part of the time involved in map-making. During these absences, Yoï had to deal with the business of the farm, which had been worked for years by an elderly couple. She later described one terrifying experience:

It was during the last year of the war… that the old couple who had farmed our fields died almost in the same month, and we had to choose whoever we could get. A much younger man who, unfortunately, had what his wife called a nervous temperament, came to do the work. My husband was at the front and I had to look after the new man who shared with us, half and half, under the mezzadria system. For the first month we got on pretty well, but after that trouble came. He bought a cow and sold it in ten days, having made what seemed to me to be an enormous profit. I said, "It is very wrong that such profits should be possible in war time, we ought not to use that money." I saw that it had suddenly flashed on him "she is quite mad," and from that moment he changed. He sold everything, even the children's goats, without asking my opinion, and never gave me any of the money he made by the sale of beasts, vegetables or fruit.

At this time he began to suffer from his stomach; his wife said he had never been well, but now he often had great pain, and the doctor who came to see him told me that he was dying of a tumour, and also that he was very excitable and possibly dangerous. It was then, too, that I was told secretly, so as not to bring his wrath on the head of the speaker, that he had been sent away from another place after flying at his employer with a knife. Here was a dilemma. From that moment I could only sleep in snatches as he had mumbled something about climbing windows at night, and at every sound I crawled out of bed clutching my revolver.

Everyone was kind; the Carabinieri came nearly every day to see how things were going, but nothing could be done; I could not leave home with such young children, and the man was too ill to be worried; there was, besides, a law that no peasant could be sent away without a long law suit. It had to be borne, as others bore the Zeppelins and bombs.

But the breaking point came at last. One dark night at two o'clock, I heard what could only have been the scraping of a jemmy at a back door. Shoeless, I ran to the room of the housemaid and asked her to come with me to listen. She was the daughter of the peasants who had died, and was a perfect type of Italian girl, both in looks and character. She showed much courage and followed me. A moment after we heard a great noise as if bricks had given way. She whispered to me, "Go to the window and shoot." I ran to the window, shot three times, and then shouted "Help, help." In the meantime she listened at a back window and heard someone running into the thick bushes that grow all round the house. I looked towards the peasant's house, quite close to ours, thinking they would surely open a window; but there was no sign. From a window of a little house on the road below a man's voice called out "What is it?" I said "We are women alone, please come and help us to see if anyone is still about." The voice said, "I will come at once," and the window was shut. The door of that little house, however, did not open, and next morning I heard that the owner thought it wiser, as shooting was going on, to stop safely in bed. Beppina – I must write of her by name for she is one of the dearest recollections of ten years' life in Italy – Beppina and I, too much upset to be able to sleep, sat together in silence, waiting for the dawn.

We never knew if it had been a real attempt at burglary, or if our nervous friend had done it to frighten us, but from that time till the end of that year I could see nothing amusing in anything that happened. During his last months, for till the last week of his life he could prowl about the bushes, I did not have a moment free of anxiety.

At last, on a windy night in January, gravel was thrown up at my window, and on opening it, first putting out all the lights behind me, I found his wife standing below holding a lantern. She asked if I could send for the priest as her husband was dying. I dared not, then, think what it must have meant for her to know there was the end of curses and beatings; he had suffered cruelly, we had all suffered together, and was it not for us to ask his forgiveness for, perhaps, some lack of patience and sympathy?[79]

By the time the war ended in 1918, Antonio was working for the Royal Air Force in Italy, helping with surveying and map-making. Yoï and Antonio's third son, Grato, had been born in November 1917.

In May 1918, Yoï was approached by the essayist and critic Emilio Cecchi, who wanted her to send him interesting items from the English papers for him to review. She agreed enthusiastically:

Dear Signor Cecchi
Of course I shall be delighted to help & please look upon me as your secretary here in Florence & tell me of anything I can do.

*I am writing today to have some more papers sent me from England. Would
you tell me more clearly what kind of news you want & could you send me a copy
of the giornalino so that I can see what kind of things it needs.*[80]

Over the next few months, this correspondence was to develop into a
friendship, and *Signor Cecchi* soon became *Amico*. He too was involved
in some form of war work, and Yoï sent cuttings for him with Antonio
when he went back after being home on leave. In her letters to Emilio
Cecchi she shared her feelings about the war and also corrected his
English:

*I am busy with the garden – just as if something forced me to keep close to growing
plants – these & little children are necessary for me as an artist – my soul must be
a constructive one – When I think too long of the war I want to kill myself I have
such a horror of pain, mental & physical.*

*Thank goodness I get good news of Nello [Antonio] – Do write again – Your
letter was splendid – only one real fault. Si dice "but as I remember you prefer
English" – not "but as I remind."*[81]

Emilio Cecchi was in London by December 1918. Yoï wrote playfully
about the possibility of meeting him there the following spring:

*I hope you may still be in London when I get there – perhaps in April – & we'll go
to Pagani's together & eat minestrone & talk Italian & have great fun in a strange
country – Non è vero! I hope so much that Nello will be able to be there with me
at least a part of the time.* [82]

and of her first flight:

*… By the way I have news for you – last week I flew over Florence in a fighting
aeroplane – I wore the flying kit of one of the pilots – & when I showed the
photograph of the pilot & me together to the cook, she said, "Which is you, Signora?"*

*We went at about 100 miles an hour – I felt as if I had flown into a new
element – something more rough than the waves of a stormy sea & that and the great
noise took away all the sense of what I felt before flying would mean – I enjoyed it
thoroughly & oddly enough liked the danger.*

*… Do write again soon – I shall be alone again after the 28th December &
will want letters to cheer me up, as I hate Nello going away – this has been one of
our happiest times together.*

*Don't let anyone take you to the geological museum – I want to take you there
– It almost belongs to me, as I don't believe anyone else ever goes there. You will love
the wonderful colours of the stones.*[83]

By now, she is sharing her impressions of others with him:

*Yesterday at a luncheon I sat next to a real type of antifeminist man – large & loud
– an American oddly enough. He spoke crushingly about women & parliament &
I thought "you speak like that because you know you are really weak & think to
force your thoughts on others by shouting against women". When men know they
are strong, they are good friends to women & understand them better – Don't you
think so?*

*Your letters interest me very much – it is delightful to get your impressions of
new people & a new city, though by the way you don't say much about London –
Have you been too busy thinking to see it? Is the weather too bad?… & lots more
questions about everything that you can answer without my asking them. I wonder
when you will come back. I hope you will go to the Zoo – & I hope you will see
something of the English country – it's very lovely & not like anything else – the
villages would delight you.*[84]

In January 1919, she describes the departure of some of the planes that
had been based in Florence and were now returning to England:

*We have been living in a whirl of flying men & lately of Red Cross nurses – I wish
you had been here with us yesterday to see the departure of five enormous fighting
aeroplanes & three smaller ones – The noise was tremendous and when they rose
all the Campo di Marte leaves & papers rose up after them – I half expected to find
myself with Nello & Fosco halfway to the moon.*

*… Nello is still here on duty to the last of the Flying Corps left here. He gets
back to the Wing next week & hopes to be home by the end of February.*[85]

And by February, she is offering advice on shopping in London:

The address of the shoe shop for your children is Daniel Neal & Sons, 126 Kensington High Street. Tell them Signora Maraini of Florence told you to go there.

Mrs Cecchi came yesterday & I promised her to send you this address.

… It was nice of you to send me a picture card – I have a childlike fondness for them & they remind one too, often, of places one loves.[86]

And in her last surviving letter to Emilio Cecchi, we learn her opinion of the Florentines:

I have no news for you – I have been 3 days in bed with febbre – the cold & damp & Florence in general – but I mean to buck up as I live for the time when I can get to England. Your wife looked well yesterday & seemed cheerful though she has had servant worries – such as one only has in Florence – Dear Emilio Cecchi – how can it be that you are a Florentine – I can't believe it. You are everything that is the opposite of narrow, cruel & materialistic.

Yrs ever

Y. M.[87]

The Early Twenties

In 1915, just before Italy entered the war, Yoï's husband, Antonio Maraini, had been appointed art critic of the Roman newspaper *La Tribuna*. This was to be the first of a number of appointments in which he would become established not only as an artist but also as a critic and administrator in the wider field of Italian artistic activity. Once the interruption caused by the war was behind him, he returned to sculpture with enthusiasm. Yoï features in many of his works from this period, sometimes with one or other of the children, for example, in pieces such as *Maternità* and *Gruppo di famiglia*.

The two boys were generally looked after by "Nana", whose real name was Marie Pugh. By 1921, she had moved to Great Yarmouth, but Fosco wrote to her occasionally and some years later visited her in Norfolk.

Far away in Johannesburg, Yoï's father, Andrew Frederick Crosse, was making a name for himself. In 1909, he had patented an improved method of extracting gold and silver from the crushed ore,[88] and the following year he patented an improved method for the fine grinding of ores.[89] Now in 1921, writing in the *Journal of the Chemical, Metallurgical and Mineralogical Society of South Africa*, he announced his discovery of a new mineral:

> One of the most interesting mineralogical discoveries in the Transvaal is an extraordinarily rich nickel ore… This ore is as far as I am able to judge a new and undescribed mineral… I should like to call it 'Trevorite' after Major T. G. Trevor, Mining Inspector for the Pretoria District.[90]

In London, the forthcoming marriage of Yoï's daughter, Wilma, was announced.

The marriage arranged between F. H. Bernhard, eldest son of Mr. and Mrs. Bernhard, of Windmill House, Shirley, Surrey, and Wilma, daughter of Captain Buckley, of Claradine, Pendine, South Wales, will take place on September 17 in London.[91]

The bride has only one parent in this announcement – obviously, Yoï had completely ceased to exist as far as the Buckley family was concerned.

Yoï's great-aunt Theresa Berkeley died in London on 13 December 1921 at the age of eighty-four. When Yoï had first arrived from Hungary to live with her grandmother Cornelia, it had been Theresa who had acted as housekeeper to enable Cornelia to devote her time to her writing. Yoï had later dedicated *A Child Went Forth* to her great-aunt, for whom she had great affection. She would be sadly missed.

Yoï continued to write, submitting a regular series of articles to the London weekly *Saturday Review* under the heading *A Woman's Causerie*, a causerie being "A conversation or short written article, casual in tone, but serious in content". The first article appeared on 6 May 1922. She produced one nearly every week for the first year, after which they appeared slightly less frequently and finally ended in January 1924. The subjects ranged widely, including travel, people she had known, children's books, and even one on the nature of married love.

In 1922, Yoï's fourth book was published by Collins, in London. This time she uses the name "Yoï Maraini", although on the title page, "Yoï Pawlowska" appears in brackets underneath. *In a Grain of Sand* is a series of sketches of Florentine life, illustrated with six drawings by Antonio. Yoï's introduction says:

If there is any value in what I write it is because I have known Florence from a point of view rare for a stranger. The life that has interested me has not been that lived in the beautiful villas on the hills – an incomplete, cosmopolitan life such as any of the large hotels in the world can show – but I have been privileged to know something of the working people, and it is of these, chiefly, that I have written.[92]

Back in Britain, Wilma, too, was writing. In the summer of 1923, she published a volume of poetry, which the *Llanelly Guardian* described as a "delightful little volume… full of charm and rich in promise".[93]

In April 1923, Yoï's solicitor and friend, Edward Heron-Allen, was on holiday in Florence with his wife, Nour. Yoï visited them at their hotel and later introduced them to many of her circle of friends. On 21 April, the Heron-Allens took the tram out to Ricorboli, where they spent a very rainy afternoon with Yoï and Antonio at the farm, including a visit to Antonio's studio. The Heron-Allens left Florence on 26 April, but the two families kept in touch for many years to come.[94]

In Italy at this time there was serious political division. A majority of the population had been opposed to the country's involvement in the recent war, and there was now a violent polarisation of political attitudes within the country. In March 1919, a new political movement had been founded in Milan, known as *Fascismo*, a name derived from the Italian word *fascio*, which means "bundle" or "union". Within a couple of years, *il duce* (the leader), Benito Mussolini, was in parliament at the head of a group of Fascist deputies, and before the end of 1922 he had been invited by King Victor Emanuel III to form a government.

So much has been written over the years about the Italian Fascists and their violent methods that it is hard for us in the 21st century to understand how they were seen at the time. In Europe generally the Italian Fascist movement was widely welcomed as the saviour of a divided and chaotic Italy. For example, this advertisement appeared in *The Times* on 4 January 1924:

> *A MESSAGE FROM MUSSOLINI*
> *In this week's issue of The Spectator the great Prime Minister of Italy – "the pilot who weathered the storm and took the mighty ship of State triumphantly into harbour" – speaks to the British people of the hopes and aims of Fascismo, the strange new force that has electrified all Italy.*[95]

On 26 March 1924, Yoï was at the Chigi Palace in Rome to interview *il duce* himself for the *Saturday Review*. At the time, the country was in the middle of an election campaign in which vote rigging, violence and even murder were employed by the Fascists in order to ensure they were returned to power. Behind the scenes, Mussolini encouraged the violence, believing that people would only respect leaders of whom they were afraid. But when he granted interviews to foreign journalists, he played the part of a civilised intellectual, a gifted linguist and talented musician who also loved poetry. Yoï was certainly not alone in being completely taken in by this façade – above everything else, Mussolini was a talented actor. Denis Mack Smith, in his impressive biography of Mussolini, describes him as:

> *… a dissimulator, an exhibitionist who changed his role from hour to hour to suit the occasion.*[96]

Yoï was totally convinced by the performance he gave for her benefit:

> *Up to the moment when I saw him seated, and before I had seen his face clearly, or had heard his voice speaking of something that interested him, I had not felt in the least impressed. Other great men, in other beautiful rooms, receive journalists, and give their opinions on events as if what they said had an eternal significance. But as he was speaking I realised with a rush that I was in the presence of a man different from all other men, a really great man, a man of education in the widest sense of the word, with a stupendous brain combined with a rare quality of imagination and, suddenly, I was afraid. I was facing a solitary spirit, a vital force whom one could only hope to know, even remotely, through a flash of intuition. He has yet another gift, as I, soon found out, and one which every Anglo-Saxon values, that is a keen sense of humour. This will, probably, help to keep alive in him that self-criticism, the loss of which means the loss of a man's greatness.*[97]

It is difficult for the modern reader to keep this sort of thing in perspective. With the advantage of hindsight, it is hard to credit such apparent naivety. But it is important to remember that, at the time, the press in Italy was either under the direct control of the Fascists, or had been gradually cowed by threats of violence. The only publicly expressed opinions were all enthusiastically supportive of Italy's remarkable achievements, and these were apparently wholly due to one man – Mussolini. It would be many years before a more realistic picture would emerge: that of an extremely corrupt society where appearance was more important than reality and where in all cases the ends justified the often-violent means. But for the moment, Mussolini had Yoï in the palm of his hand:

… he pointed to a few books close to him on the table. I would have given a good deal to have read their titles, but these were hidden by papers. Mussolini then went on to talk of the arts, and as he was speaking, and got more and more interested in the subject, he got up and came to the side of the table. Counting on the fingers of his hand, he said:

"This is how I place the importance of the various arts. I mean, of course, their importance to me. First, music." Here he held and shook his thumb. "Yes, music first of all and above all. Then architecture, then poetry, then sculpture, and then painting and so on. And I put music first because it is the most easily communicated. When I take my violin and play I get, at once, into touch with the music of whatever country it may be; I get into the soul of that music, it is mine, a part of me. You know what Shakespeare says of music – and Shelley too."

As he spoke of Shelley he took up a book and held it in his hands looking down at it.

"Shelley is music."

I must here say, what few people know, that Mussolini plays the violin well and that, among the English poets, Shelley is the one that appeals to the mystic in him. These things he did not tell me himself. The first I was told by a friend of his who had often heard him play, the second I judged, myself, was the reason of his fondness for Shelley. This love of Shelley may, perhaps, throw a light on the secret of his vast power over his countrymen, and over all who come in contact with him: Mussolini is an idealist. He asks men to make sacrifices for an ideal because with his spirit's clear vision he sees that we must give all to gain all.

He is ready to give even his life for the cause he holds dear, that is, the work of Fascism as a constructive force for the restoration of discipline and devotion as an ideal of life.

As time was passing I hurried, unwillingly, I must confess, for Mussolini has vivid and fresh views on the arts, to ask him other questions.

"I feel certain that the readers of the Saturday Review would be most interested to know your point of view with regard to the economic future of Europe in general, and how far you think that the working-class public is likely to go on demanding a rate of wages which is entirely uneconomic; in other words, how long are people likely to expect to be paid more than they are actually earning?"

The President, with clear wide-open eyes, looked for a moment thoughtfully in front of him. Then he began. I quote him word for word:

"I believe that Europe is already on the way to restoration. The problem that the war left was not an economic problem, but a spiritual one. War impresses the spirit of a people even more profoundly than it lacerates their economic structure, and it is vividly reflected in the education of the masses, in their attitude to work and in their manner of living. There has been in Europe, and for the matter of that, also in America and in Japan, a crisis of the workers which we may call a moral crisis, and this crisis which devastated the regime of economic production was used by the revolutionary elements of the whole world for their own ends. This crisis has in Italy been entirely overcome. With their good sense, and with their experience of many centuries, the Italian people after a short but dark period of disorder turned to a more normal conception of life, to more rigid habits of work, and to a tranquillity of spirit which promises, to-day, that the economic condition of Italy will help to surmount the difficulties of the general situation. For eighteen months now there have been no strikes in Italy, even though the conditions of living are as difficult here, as anywhere else, and in spite of the fact that the restrictive laws of emigration, in some of the Transatlantic countries, have reduced, in a very grave manner, our capacity of finding work. And yet Italy is, today, the country that, in Europe, enjoys the greatest stability."

And she sums him up in her final paragraph:

It is difficult, without exaggerating, to speak of all the divers qualities of this wonderful man. But we are apt, in speaking of his strength, to forget wide humanity. And what is strength without this, far greater, quality born in great souls from hardship, disillusion and suffering and nourished by hope and belief?

Yoï's article, *A Talk with Mussolini*, appeared in the *Saturday Review* on 5 April 1924, after being prominently advertised in *The Times* earlier in the week.

Family and Friends

Yoï's former husband, James Buckley, died in Montreux on 11 March 1924. He was fifty-five. Their two children, Wilma and Ifor, now twenty-five and twenty, had kept in touch with their mother over the years and usually met Yoï when she visited England. Wilma was married and a published poet, while Ifor, after a brief spell on a farm in Norfolk, was articled to a brewing firm in Reading to prepare him for his later involvement in the family firm.

In the summer of 1924, Yoï first met the woman who was to become her closest friend. Dorothy Nevile Lees had been born in Wolverhampton in 1880, where her father was a successful merchant and manufacturer of enamelled tin and Japan ware. When Dorothy was still very young, the family moved to Tettenhall, Staffordshire, and it was there that Dorothy spent her childhood. Her father, William Lees, had travelled widely; her mother, Rose, had spent much of her childhood in Livorno; and both parents loved Italy and spoke the language fluently. Dorothy grew up surrounded by Italian art, history and culture.

When her father's business suffered financial losses around 1898, the family remained in Tettenhall but moved to a smaller house. Dorothy now began to press her father to allow her to visit Italy. Finally, he agreed. She arrived in Florence in 1903, determined to make an independent living by whatever means she could but with the long-term aim of becoming a professional writer. Initially, she worked as an *au pair*, then later in a typing and translation agency in central Florence. She also wrote two books about life in Tuscany: *Scenes and Shrines in Tuscany*, and *Tuscan Feasts and Tuscan Friends*, which were both published in 1907. [98]

While still a child in England, Dorothy had seen the great English actress Ellen Terry as Portia. Now she heard that Ellen Terry's son, the theatre producer and designer Edward Gordon Craig, was living in Florence and was looking for someone who could act as his secretary and help in the preparation of articles in English. Before long, she was working with Gordon Craig to the exclusion of everything else. In March 1908, they published the first edition of *The Mask*, an English-language journal of the theatre. Most of the articles were written by either Gordon Craig or Dorothy herself, under a variety of pseudonyms. In March 1913, with Dorothy taking care of the administration, Craig opened his School of the Art of the Theatre, in the *Arena Goldoni* in the *Via dei Serragli*. But in August 1914, war was declared, and the school never reopened after the summer break.

Dorothy continued to work for Craig, with whom she was very much in love, as well as being passionately committed to his ideals and visions of a "New Theatre". In September 1917, she gave birth to their son, David Lees. Gordon Craig already had four children with his wife, May, whom he had left in 1898, three children with the violinist Elena Fortuna Meo, and two more with the dancer Isadora Duncan.

The Mask continued to be produced at somewhat irregular intervals after the war. In May 1924, Dorothy sent a copy to Yoï and Antonio, presumably as part of an attempt to increase its circulation, which was never high. Yoï wrote to thank her:

Sunday
Dear Miss Nevile Lees
　　Thank you very much for The Mask. How interesting it is & so beautifully edited & printed.
　　I am so looking forward to seeing you very soon as I am not going to Rome till later – but for the moment I am going through the worry of changing governesses & cannot make plans –
　　Yrs sincerely
　　Yoï Maraini [99]

A few days later, Yoï wrote again to Dorothy enclosing her subscription of 50 lire and a cutting from the *Saturday Review* with a very favourable review of *The Mask*. In a later note, she discussed the possibility of them meeting for tea and says she longed to hear Dorothy's "soft voice" again. Over the next few weeks, their initially formal acquaintance developed into a close friendship that was to last for years. The two women had a great deal in common and were very unlike most of the English community living in Florence at the time. They were both of a similar age – Dorothy was forty-four, Yoï was forty-seven – and each had a son aged seven, although of course Yoï also had an older son, Fosco, who was by now twelve.

Yoï's letters to Dorothy cover a period of roughly ten years from 1924 onwards. They have survived thanks to Dorothy's habit of filing everything, both business and personal correspondence. Many of them were hastily scrawled notes, perhaps inviting Dorothy and David to tea. Others were written while Yoï was visiting London, which she tried to do every year, and contain complaints on the weather, or comments about the people she has met.

Among Yoï and Antonio's other friends at this time were the English writer Aldous Huxley and his wife, Maria. They lived in Florence for a few years in the early 1920s. Maria Huxley was helping another English writer, D. H. Lawrence, by typing the manuscript of what would become *Lady Chatterley's Lover*. The Lawrences and the Huxleys would sometimes visit Yoï and Antonio at the Ricorboli farm, where such a visit meant that Fosco had to become less of a savage for the occasion:

> *Going barefoot, on normal summer days, was allowed, perhaps even encouraged: but visits were no laughing matter, and brought out in mother a certain Nordic hardness. "Now, you just go upstairs and put on your shoes. I'm not joking. What will the Huxleys say, if they find a wild tartar around the house, eh?"* [100]

As a rule, Aldous Huxley never gave interviews, but he made an exception for Yoï just before he and Maria left for a visit to India towards the end of 1925. *A Talk with Aldous Huxley* was published in the June 1926 edition of *The Bermondsey Book*. It begins:

Aldous Huxley took a copy of Butler's "Analogy" – a favourite book of his – from my bookshelf and, standing by a window, read aloud from it a passage that amused him. I had been wondering if I dared ask him a question – he is reserved and hates advertisement – when seeing that he was laughing, I screwed up my courage to say, "Do you mind if I interview you?"

One of Aldous Huxley's most charming characteristics is an old-fashioned politeness. He smiled down at me, "Of course, if you want to."

"Well, then I will go up to your house to do so because I am certain that an interview, to be properly done, must take place at the home of the victim."

The next day I climbed the hill of Santa Margherita in Montici, in the outskirts of Florence; at the top of it found myself in the garden of the villa that Aldous Huxley describes so vividly in his story of "The Young Archimedes" in his book "The Little Mexican".

He says: "Stripped of its dark woods, plated, terraced, and tilled almost to the mountain tops, the Tuscan landscape is humanised and safe. Sometimes upon those who live in the midst of it there comes a longing for some place that is solitary, inhuman, lifeless or peopled only with alien life. But the longing is soon satisfied and one is glad to return to the civilised and submissive scene."

Aldous Huxley was standing at the end of his garden playing with his little son Matthew, both clearly silhouetted against a grey sky. They had not seen me as I walked in at the open gate, and I stopped, for a moment, to look at Aldous as if I had seen him for the first time. He is very tall, with dark hair brushed back from a pale face. His eyes are large, a deep grey, and he wears, always, glasses with broad tortoiseshell rims; he has a charming, humorous smile and is, above everything else, most distinguished-looking. He walks with loose easy movements, and his dress, though not in any way peculiar, is somehow different from that of other people, or it may be that it looks different, because he is different. Clothes are mysteriously chameleon-like. In any place, in any crowd he would stand out as remarkable and not only because of his height; he looks what he is, a scholar, a dreamer, and a poet. When he saw me he came forward, and after we had spoken a few words, I looked past him to the olive trees in the valley below, and at the pointing cypresses.

"It is always strange to find you, such a Londoner, in such Italian surroundings."

Aldous Huxley, leading the way back into the house, looked back at me.

"Well, you see I do not agree with Dr. Johnson – I prefer climate to polite society. And I believe also it is a disadvantage to have what is commonly known as advantages – they tend to keep one from reality."[101]

Later, Yoï wrote to Huxley's literary agents – James B. Pinker and Sons – asking them to sell the interview in America for her.[102]

Yoï continued to write. 1925 saw the publication by Methuen of *Little Dressmakers in Love:* another collection of short descriptive or narrative pieces about the life of the Florentine people.

On 8 December 1925, Yoï's father, Andrew Frederick Crosse, died in Cape Town at the age of seventy-three. His second wife, Frances Charlotte, was with him. In the letters that have survived from this period, Yoï does not mention her father's death. One wonders whether relations between them may have been difficult, perhaps because of his remarriage, or maybe Yoï's affair with Roy Kennard. Andrew's widow returned to England in 1926 and went to live with her unmarried sister Mina Jennings in Exmouth, Devon. She died there in 1931.

Early in 1925, Antonio had bought an eighteenth century farmhouse, *Torre di Sopra*, in the *Via Benedetto Castelli* on the hill to the south of Florence. He commissioned Cecil Pinsent, the English architect who had worked with Geoffrey Scott on the Berensons' villa of *I Tatti,* to make it into a modern family home, with studio facilities in a converted barn. By the end of 1926, the house was ready. Yoï later described it in an illustrated article in the *Architectural Review:*

> The outside of the house has not been touched; the three large arches facing the stone-paved aia, where corn was beaten, but where now grass and flowers grow between the crevices, form a loggia where carts used to be kept, and is now a delightfully sheltered place for meals and work. Inside, though the rooms are comfortable, according to the most modern ideas of comfort, very little structural alteration was needed…
>
> … Two very large studios have been added close to the house – one with a miniature railway line – so that the artist can see his work, for monuments, in the open air. The garden is made by olive trees growing close up to the house, and everything has been done to preserve the surroundings as much as possible in keeping with the simple beauty of a Tuscan farmhouse, still in its original setting.[103]

Yoï's children Wilma and Ifor Buckley were keen travellers, and even after Wilma's marriage to Frank Bernhard in 1921, she would still make long sea voyages with her brother. In 1926, Ifor and Wilma set off together on a round-the-world journey. They sailed from Southampton on the *S. S. Tainui*, heading for Australia and New Zealand. Yoï spent some time with them when the ship visited Naples. They were back in England by the autumn.

In London's West End, C. B. Cochran's 1926 Revue was receiving good reviews. The cast at the London Pavilion included Hermione Baddeley, Florence Desmond and Ernest Thesiger, with choreography by Léonide Massine. Later in its run, the American comedian Will Rogers would join the company. Also in the cast was a twenty-one-year-old actress and singer whose professional name was Thalia Barberova but who was better known to her family and friends in Streatham as Barbara Pauline Long. On 21 October 1926, *The Times* carried the announcement of an engagement between Yoï's son Ifor Buckley and Thalia Barberova.[104] Ifor and Barbara were married on 6 January 1927 in Marylebone Register Office. The *South Wales Press*, Llanelli's weekly newspaper, gave a full report:

AN ACTRESS BRIDE
LLANELLY DIRECTOR'S MARRIAGE

Mr Gabriel James Ifor Buckley, the twenty-two year old Director of Buckley's Brewery Limited, was married to a popular young West End actress, Miss Thalia Barberova at St. Marylebone Register Office on Thursday.

The Bridegroom is a son of the late Captain James Buckley of the Imperial Yeomanry, and nephew of Lady Hughes-Morgan, wife of Sir David Hughes-Morgan, Bart JP, and Chairman of the Western Mail Limited.

The bride, who is known in private life as Miss Barbara Pauline Long, although only twenty-one has appeared in several West End productions, including the 'Punch Bowl', 'Still Dancing' and Cochran's Revue of 1926.

Miss Barbara was wearing a beautiful squirrel wrap over a rose dress and a small hat to match. She was described on the register as the daughter of Mr. Albert George Long, Inspecting Engineer, Admiralty. Among those present were the bridegroom's stepmother Loïs Buckley who was one of the witnesses. The honeymoon will be spent on the Riviera.

The Bride and Groom had intended to travel to Paris by air but as it was doubtful whether the fog which prevailed in the morning would lift sufficiently to make the journey possible, they abandoned this prospect and instead left London by the 11 o'clock boat train from Victoria. The machine by which they intended to travel did, in fact, leave Croydon at the scheduled time.[105]

After a month on the Riviera, the young couple returned by sea from Marseilles to London.

On 4 May 1928, *The Times* reported on the opening of the 16th International Art Exhibition of Venice, the *Biennale*, the previous day:

At 9.30 twelve gilded State barges of the City of Venice, with a number of State gondolas, left the Municipal Palace carrying the Podestà, Count Orsi, the Duke of Bergamo, who represented the King, and Count Volpi, the Minister of Finance, representing the Government. Flags and tapestries were hung from the balconies of the old patrician palaces on both sides of the Canal, and the picturesque water pageant was favoured by brilliant sunshine.

The formal opening ceremony took place at the entrance to the Exhibition, where speeches were delivered by Count Orsi and Count Volpi. Then the Duke of Bergamo, the authorities, and the guests, led by Signor Maraini, the new Secretary of the Exhibition, visited the various halls and pavilions.[106]

Antonio had been appointed Secretary of the Venice *Biennale* in October 1927, with an office in the Doge's Palace. It was a position he was to hold for many years. Dorothy moved into *Torre di Sopra* for a week or two to keep an eye on things there so that Yoï could be with him in Venice. Antonio had invited Edward Gordon Craig to send some work as part of an exhibit of theatrical design, but ultimately he felt unable to contribute.

Gordon Craig's mother, Ellen Terry, died in July 1928 at her home at Smallhythe in Kent. The funeral took place there on Tuesday 24 July. Yoï wrote to Dorothy from Cortina, on her way home from a visit to London to see various editors, one of a number of letters over the years in which she tells how she has been trying to encourage them to take Dorothy's work as well as her own.

Dear Dorothy – I thought of you when Ellen Terry died & wished you & David could have been at the funeral – It must have been so gay & just right – exactly as she wished it to be. I couldn't go cos my train left at 2 – but a friend came to see me off – who had been there – & told me about it & that everyone was in bright colours & there was nothing gloomy – I expect you have heard all about it from G[ordon] C[raig].

When I see you – which I hope will be soon – I can tell you all I tried to do for your work. I had a long talk with Mr. Braithwaite – he kept off the subject of D[avid] – but I felt he knew and was sympathetic – About that talk we must have a long talk. I also spoke to the Queen editor about you & the Architectural Review. Hastings (the A. Rev. editor) said that as a rule they ask Mr. Craig to do theatre news for them, but I said if he was busy or didn't want to do it – you were the very person to write on the art of the theatre – It's no good if they write to you about all this we must meet as soon as we can & I can tell you everything – The heat must be too too awful – I can't tell you how often I have wished that you and David were here & out of it – though I loathe hotel life & feel that all these ghastly people spoil a most lovely place. Here there is not even a village – we go straight on to the Cristallo one of the loveliest mountains in the Dolomites & the wild flowers are most beautiful. I can't do much walking yet as the journey to London & back & London, with 90 in the shade, pretty well did for me. Just think I lived in London in chiffon dresses & couldn't even bear a belt to keep up my stockings – so rolled them! The visit was a huge success. I have got the exhibition arranged for the Roman woman artist & have heaps of orders for articles on Italian decorative art. Do forgive the pencil. I have only ink enough to write the address. I hope to be back on about the 20th*. The card enclosed is for David with my love. Do let me hear that you are not feeling the heat too much – It must get cooler soon. Yrs with love Yoï* [107]

In November, an appeal was launched to raise funds for a suitable memorial to Ellen Terry:

Those who admired and loved Dame Ellen Terry will be glad to know that it is proposed to acquire, as a public possession, "Small Hythe Place," the fine old Tudor timbered house, between Tenterden and Rye, where she spent the greater part of the last twenty-five years of her life, and where she died; that two rooms shall be kept much as they were in her lifetime, preserving the atmosphere of simplicity which surrounded her, and keeping intact the relics of her personal belongings; and that a third room shall be furnished and used as a library, chiefly of books relating to the drama and theatre, of which Dame Ellen's own collection, which contains many volumes annotated by Sir Henry Irving and herself, would form the nucleus together with a small museum of theatrical relics of historical interest; and also to adapt a barn adjoining the house as a theatre where small festivals can be held.

It is estimated that the scheme, of which Sir Johnston Forbes Robertson is Chairman, and Lady Maud Warrender Hon. Treasurer, can be adequately carried out and endowed for £15,000, and it is proposed to make a public appeal for this sum.[108]

On 20 March 1929, Lady Warrender herself gave a talk at the British Institute in Florence to support the Ellen Terry Memorial Fund. Yoï was an enthusiastic fundraiser, liaising with the Director of the Institute, Harold Goad. She wrote to Dorothy:

I have arranged with Mr Goad that the money is to be paid in lire to the British Institute marked "for Ellen Terry Memorial". He has given 50 lire & so have I – but anything from 5 lire up will be welcome – don't you think. I have sent a bunch of these leaflets to Reggie Temple & hope he will rouse a few people. Darling Ellen Terry – all loveliness & light & beautiful English Spring – Nothing could be a better memorial for her than an English cottage with its garden filled with flowers – Nothing can ever match her generosity of soul – Oh I have some lovely recollections of her.

… I do hope Dorothy it won't mean a lot of extra work for you trying to get people to subscribe – but if it is I know it means a work of love – [109]

And again a few days later:

Lady Maud's talk & concert is on Wednesday at the British Institute. Mind you come & get people to come. I have got a subscription from Lady Headfort (Rosie Boote as was). She hadn't even heard of the memorial in London! [110]

The actress and dancer Rosie Boote had created something of a scandal when the young Marquess of Headfort saw her appearing at the Gaiety Theatre, London, and proposed to her. They were married in April 1901.

Yoï's son Ifor Buckley was now a director of Buckley's Brewery Ltd. and was taking a more active role in its management, but he still found time for extensive trips abroad. In January 1929, he and his wife, Barbara, took a cruise to the West Indies and back. Later that same year, in June, Ifor and a friend embarked on the *Port Fairy* at Tilbury, heading for Australia. Barbara came to see him off. This voyage was to prove disastrous, as the *Llanelly Mercury* later reported:

> *Mr. Buckley was accompanied by his friend, Mr. Richard Hunter. Shortly after leaving England he contracted septic blood poisoning, and this was followed within a few days by erysipelas. His condition steadily became more serious and on the 9th instant a wireless message was sent to his relatives that in view of his condition it was proposed to land him at Port Said.*
>
> *On the 10th Mr. Buckley's condition became much worse and was accompanied by a high temperature. With the intention of soothing the patient and easing his pain, the ship's doctor administered morphia on the night of the 11th. He expressed the opinion to Mr. Hunter that as a result Mr. Buckley would sleep for at least twelve hours.*
>
> *At various times during the night the patient was visited by Mr. Hunter, the doctor and the Master of the ship, and on each occasion it was found that he was in a deep sleep. At 5 a.m. on the 12th Mr. Buckley's cabin door was found open and to the consternation of all on board, the unfortunate gentleman was nowhere to be found.*
>
> *He had previously wandered from his cabin and was discovered, to his own amazement, lying in the smoke room. It would seem, therefore, that while in a state of delirium he left his cabin and must have fallen overboard.*[111]

At the time, the ship was in the Mediterranean, heading for Egypt, and roughly equidistant from Crete and the coast of Libya.

The news of Ifor's death reached Yoï in Florence a day or two later. She scribbled an anguished note to Dorothy:

> *Saturday [15 June 1929]*
>
> *Dorothy, I am absolutely broken. Today's post tells me that my boy Ifor is dead – I can't write anything or say anything.*
>
> *Life is too, too horribly cruel – always.*[112]

And a day or so later:

Yesterday I heard the details and went nearly mad.[113]

In spite of the medical evidence, Yoï became convinced that Ifor's death was suicide and that she was to blame because she had abandoned him when he was young. Fosco later was to write that it changed her forever:

[she] unfortunately gave it an entirely personal interpretation... The possibility of the suicide of her son, which secretly, and totally without reason, she felt was her fault, affected her cruelly. He and his mother had been very close, he wrote often, there was always a photo of him on her bedside table. "I should never have left him" she repeated again and again, in tears.

But if the explicit expression of those thoughts was rare... the hidden feeling became almost an obsession for her. From the day she heard the news she was greatly changed. She lost her sparkle of vitality, her deep interest in human beings as such, in their classes, ages, conditions, languages, religions, professions, faces, and everything that happened to them.[114]

Eight months after Ifor's death, his widow, Barbara, gave birth to a baby girl. She was registered as Barbara Anne Buckley, but from the age of about fourteen was always known as Angela.

The Thirties

The political scene in Italy was becoming more and more oppressive, but artists of all sorts managed to carry on more or less as usual. Indeed, with a considerable amount of state sponsorship available, many felt they were very fortunate to be living under a Fascist regime. Antonio seems to have adopted a fairly pragmatic approach to politics. Fosco was to write of his father, many years later:

> … [he] was not a fan of the system, he joined late and almost on the sly, as if he was trying to get to his seat at the theatre after curtain-up, walking on tiptoe and trying to get noticed as little as possible.
>
> On the other hand he was a true believer – and this made him an uncomfortable and difficult opponent. The few times that he spoke… on these issues he more or less said the same thing: "You see, I am a man of order, I appreciate discipline, the completed form, both in art and in life. Mussolini has saved us from chaos and we must be grateful to him for that. Of course the man is dangerous because of the absolute power that he has over many of his followers, but I hope he will not abuse that. For now all is in good standing." And here he mentioned the reclamation of the Pontine marshes, the transformation to modern paved roads of tracks that had been dusty and cracked, or muddy (depending on the season), and so on.[115]

By 1930 the government had created a system of regional artists' syndicates, together with a coordinating body, the Fascist Syndicate of Fine Arts (*Sindacato Fascista delle Belle Arti*). Antonio was appointed its

TOP:
Fyne Court, the Crosse family home before it was destroyed by fire in 1894

RIGHT:
*Cornelia Crosse,
Yoï's grandmother, about 1876*

Theresa Berkeley, Yoï's great-aunt,
about 1876

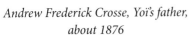

Andrew Frederick Crosse, Yoï's father,
about 1876

Emilia Pawlowski, Yoï's mother,
about 1876

Yoï, aged about 13, about 1890

The Buckley family home, Bryncaerau, Llanelli, which was built about 1896

Wilma and Yoï, about 1900

Wilma and Yoï, about 1901

James and Wilma Buckley, about 1902

Yoï's sister Gabriella, about 1904

A statuette by Antonio Maraini, Yoï with the Egyptian Idol, about 1911

Wilma and Ifor, about 1912

Antonio and Grato, about 1917

Andrew Frederick Crosse, Yoï's father, with his patented invention, about 1920

Wilma, about 1921

Yoï in fancy dress, about 1922

Yoï with Grato, in 1922

Thalia Barberova (Barbara Pauline Long) in 1925

A statuette by Antonio Maraini, Dafne,
about 1928

Sculpture by Antonio Maraini,
La Bagnante, about 1928

Torre di Sopra, Florence, about 1928

*Ifor's memorial, erected in 1931 in Holy Trinity
Church, Felinfoel, Llanelli*

Fosco in 1933

Grato in 1933

Grato, Wilma, Fosco and Yoï in 1933

Fosco and Yoï in 1934

Yoï in 1936

Yoï's grave below San Miniato del Monte, in Florence

*Yoï's headstone, carved by Antonio after her death
in 1944*

secretary. And in an article that she wrote for the *Architectural Review* in London, Yoï herself said:

> *And, thanks to the Fascist spirit, there is beginning to be less of that snobbishness that finds commendable only what is made abroad, and by strangers.* [116]

In August 1930, Fosco went with his mother to England for the first time. Initially, they stayed in London with Wilma and her husband. Yoï had meetings with various editors, while Fosco visited the British Museum and other London landmarks. Then they both went to stay at Hinchingbrooke House, near Huntingdon, with the family of Lord Sandwich, whom they had got to know in Florence.

> *We have been to Hinchingbrooke & today Fosco goes to Wilton and Cowes. Next week we run down to Wales & for the week-end to Attingham the Berwicks place in Shropshire – We have also been asked to stop at Stratford-on-Avon at the house of Shakespeare's daughter.*
>
> *I am seeing masses of people, but am rather crushed by the wet…* [117]

On their way home, they stopped for a few days in Milan and also visited Monza:

> *Dear Dorothy*
> *Thank you for writing… Monza is going to be splendid. I was there all yesterday & in the evening in a box for the Toscanini concert. After I went to the party given at the Scala for Toscanini – & had a talk with him on Respighi & Pizzetti, & their respective wives – Also with our ambassador & with Mrs Janett the American ambassadress. All very interesting. Tomorrow all day long at Monza for writing about it – On Sunday at 11 the opening. Every sort of care is being taken as the Princess is coming too – only very few people are allowed in the palace & all under supervision. I am to be in the British part & Nello, who comes today, will represent Venice. It's all amusing but I shall be glad to be home again –*
> *…It's all right about the Sphere, but Home had said he didn't want anything about the football match. When he sees your photographs he may change his mind. There is no understanding editors. One thing Dorothy, I do feel that in an atmosphere where everyone is busy & on the move one gets through a lot more*

– Florence is deadening. I met a Mrs Howel who talked about Craig – & about you – I was very careful – but she was charming about you having heard of you from someone in Rome. She represents some American papers at Genova. More when we meet.

Love to you Yoï [118]

As in this example, in many of her letters Yoï mentions being careful in her conversations about Dorothy. Presumably, English publishers would have been scandalised by the thought of an English woman living abroad and bringing up her illegitimate child, even to the point of rejecting her work if it were to become public knowledge. There is little doubt that Dorothy was entirely reliant on her writing to support herself and David – Gordon Craig seldom contributed anything and was often completely untraceable.

Many of Yoï's letters are undated and concerned with everyday matters such as the difficulties of bringing up children:

Yesterday an English friend of mine, who knows David as a little friend of Grato's, said that she is always seeing David going too fast on his bicycle, down hills, & in & out of the traffic. Two days ago a car nearly ran into him – She doesn't think he saw what a near thing it had been.

Do talk to him about it Dorothy, because I too, have sometimes begged him to look more carefully where he is going, & to go more slowly. I don't mind bothering you about this as I know you would wish to be told – It is particularly in the Piazza of Porta Romana that he is careless & going down the Viale.

Lord! What an agony they are. [119]

Other letters accompany gifts of clothes with advice on how to use them. And always sympathy and concern for the difficulties of bringing up a child as a single mother with little or no support from the father:

Here is a tiny parcel – The evening lace – gold you can wear with any slip you like & if the lace is tight – as my things often are for other people – you can put the same silk as you use for the slip down either side under the arms – The crepe de chine flouncy dress has heaps to let out – The stuff to make up has just come from Liberty & I have no time to have it made up – so do wear it to please me – The white silk slip you can use for under that – Most people only wear a slip & a pair of silk knickers under that – Some of the Romans only wear a lacy slip – and nothing else. Hence so much slimness!

The two nightgowns were given me by the friend I stay with in London – part of a bunch of 10 – I can't possibly use them all – so you must help. They'll do for rough wear – meaning if you go to the country & get your things washed any how. That first sentence might be misunderstood!

I do hope you will find the things useful. If I don't see you before I go – do remember that Nello will be here & ready to do anything for you – You do not lack friends Dorothy – but come to us first if things are difficult. We have known such rough times.

Your loving Yoï.[120]

After Ifor Buckley's death, Yoï and Wilma had asked Antonio to create a memorial to him. He designed an oval relief panel, just under a metre high, showing a sheltering angel. The inscription reads:

In loving memory of Gabriel James Ifor Buckley – Born October 16 1904 – Lost at sea June 12 1929 – This stone has been set up by his mother and sister.[121]

When it was finished, it was shipped to South Wales and installed in Holy Trinity Church, Felinfoel, Llanelli, which was the Buckley family church. It is very close to Bryncaerau, Yoï's home after her marriage to James Buckley. On her next visit to England, Yoï made a trip from London to South Wales to see the memorial in place.

Meurice Hotel, Bury Street, St. James's, London, S. W. 1.
9 August [1931]
Dear Dorothy.
Thank you for your delightful letter. It was handed to me yesterday morning as I left the hotel at 8.15 on my way to Paddington. I went to S. Wales for the day – something of a feat – to see the memorial. It looks beautiful and I am thankful to say that the Vicar, & everyone there, is delighted with it – & very proud of it too. You will know all I felt, & I was glad to be alone.[122]

In the same letter she tells of more visits to editors, and that her younger son Grato was now staying at Hinchingbrooke.

The day before I had a long talk about you to Miss MacMillan – at the offices of the Architectural Review. She has promised to help on anything you may send & was upset about the muddle about the garden Exhibition article. I told her of your work on The Mask but asked her not to speak of it as G[ordon] C[raig] & his son both write for the paper & I did not want to make difficulties for you. She is a person you too would love, young, clever, & very understanding. I hope your right ear burnt till it hurt you! On Thursday I am lunching with Mr Braithwaite & I will try to see Mr. — I can't remember his name – before I leave. I do not seem ever to have a spare moment – but I have been able to do a good deal & have work promised me, if only I have time enough to do it.

I have been taken over the new Punch building by the architect & saw some of the great ones who write for the paper. Grato is still at Hinchingbrooke – I go there on Tuesday – We come back together on Wednesday – I had meant never to go into the country – but have been obliged to do so – I took him down and stopped there then… It all takes time & there is still so much to do. Money is the difficulty – but I am trying to be careful – Everyone is terribly worried here – & in Wales the unemployment is dreadful – All the same every Miner & his wife – with 10 children – seemed.

I have been travelling by train on Saturday – eating all the time. A kind ticket collector sent me, first, alone – so the journey was really a rest.[123]

In about 1931, Antonio had suggested to the President of the Venice *Biennale*, Count Volpi di Misurata, the idea of starting a film festival in Venice. Entitled *l'Esposizione Internazionale d'Arte Cinematografica*, it took place in August 1932, with Antonio as General Secretary. This first ever film festival was very successful, attracting over 25000 spectators. Many of the greatest Hollywood stars were present, including Greta Garbo, Clark Gable, Fredric March, Wallace Beery, Norma Shearer, James Cagney, Ronald Colman, Loretta Young, John Barrymore, Joan Crawford, Vittorio De Sica and Boris Karloff. The Venice Film Festival continues to this day.

In August 1933, Yoï was back in London on what had by now become an annual visit to see editors and meet old friends:

30 August
Dearest Dorothy
I have a moment to write because I am in bed with one of my awful heads. And

today I was to have gone to the country to see a whole group of old & dear friends all together at a party at the Hyltons. I am so disappointed – Here is Beaumont's receipt. I talked to him about his books on the ballet & said I knew you'd like to see him if he came to Florence as he said he might do. –

I haven't written yet to Mr Braithwaite but will do so now – The weather after two icy days became tropical & is unbearable. Also I only took my book to Methuen on Wednesday – and am waiting to hear – You will think I have been slack about everything & everyone but I did so want to take things quietly at first. The theatres are a delight – & there are some good films – & lots of friends in London –

This is a dull letter but I cannot write now. I liked getting your lovely newsful letter – I am asking everyone "Where is G[ordon] C[raig]?" No one seems to know at all – Only one person said "living somewhere in Paris – probably with the Rose woman."

It is extraordinary how a genius can disappear – People here live at such a rate & receive so many fresh impressions that they are shock proof & life proof – It is very queer. I shall have to talk to you for hours about this – poor Dorothy!

So much love to you both Yoï[124]

Cyril W. Beaumont, a world-renowned dance historian and critic, ran a specialist dance bookshop at 75 Charing Cross Road, London W.C.2.

A fortnight later, Yoï was still in London:

13 Sept

Dear Dorothy

I have the details for you – Methuen (E. V. Lucas) has accepted the book & I must finish it at once on my return. It is being sent back to you – Please put it very carefully somewhere safe or if you prefer give it to Adams to put in the safe in his bank. You will know best – I fly to Paris on Sunday where Nello joins me & we return to Florence together on the 23 – or 24th. These last days are a frantic rush. Yesterday I had a very long talk with the woman who is secretary to the Ellen Terry fund. She has no idea where G[ordon] C[raig] is. I told her I knew a grandchild of Ellen's in Italy & she was interested. In Paris I'll go to Sylvia Beach's shop – There will be masses of things to tell you – One thing above all – that David had better stick to Italy. Work here is difficult to find. I am remembering you & talking about you for work all the time. Mr. Braithwaite

& I had a long talk he is a darling. I met Ursula. She seemed very pleased with your reports on the library. No more now. Tomorrow I go to Maugham's first night. Love Yoï[125]

Sylvia Beach was the owner of the well-known Paris bookshop, *Shakespeare and Company*, at *12 rue de l'Odéon*. She had published James Joyce's *Ulysses* in 1922. The first night Yoï refers to was *Sheppey*, by Somerset Maugham at Wyndham's Theatre, London, with a cast that included Ralph Richardson. It was to be Maugham's last play as after its production he announced that he would write no more plays.

The book that Yoï says Methuen had accepted seems never to have been published.

The 19th *Biennale* opened on 13 May 1934. By now, Antonio had overall responsibility for organising the exhibition and spent much of his time during the intervening two years selecting works to be included. *The Times* reported:

> *Since 1930 the exhibition has been organised by a committee of five, appointed by the Government, with Signor Antonio Maraini as general secretary. The system of inviting certain eminent artists and leaving to a special international jury the task of making a selection among the works sent in is no longer in existence, Signor Maraini, himself, an art critic and sculptor, makes a tour of the studios and selects what he thinks best. A greater unity is consequently obtained in the ensemble of the show as well as a higher standard in the individual works exhibited.*[126]

Sometimes the job called for considerable tact, such as when the Whitney Museum of Modern Art announced that it was withdrawing the entire American exhibit because of the inclusion, without the authorisation of the museum, of a portrait of Miss Marion Davies, the film actress, painted by a Polish artist. When *TIME Magazine* reported the matter, they seemed less than impressed with Antonio's diplomacy:

> *Nobody in Venice last week seemed to know how the trouble started but there it was – a glittering portrait of Cinema actress Marion Davies by Tade Styka, hanging, slambang, in the vestibule of the American Pavilion at the 10th Biennial Art Exhibition. Ever since the Exhibition opened in mid-May visitors thought it*

strange that this work by a Polish artist should be so prominently displayed in a U.S. collection supposedly owned entirely by the Whitney Museum of American Art. Last week, in London, Mrs. Juliana R. Force, the Whitney Museum's energetic director, thought it was so strange that she threatened to withdraw, crate and ship back to the U.S. the entire Whitney exhibit (101 pictures) unless the unauthorised Davies portrait was removed.

...

A minor official tried to smooth matters by tacking a sign under Miss Davies' portrait stating that it should not be considered a part of the U.S. exhibition... Exhibition officials, nervous as tomcats, awaited the return of Count Volpi to settle what threatened to become an international incident. Professor Maraini did not help things along much when he remarked of the Davies portrait: "It's no worse than some of the other American exhibits..."[127]

Yoï's son Fosco, meanwhile, had fallen in love with a Sicilian aristocrat. In July, in a thank you note to Dorothy Nevile Lees he told her:

I would love you to know Topazia, because she is really one of the most human and personal girls I've ever met.[128]

In September 1935, he married Topazia Alliata di Salaparuta – of whose impressive sounding name he once said, 'I felt I'd married a sound. Ours was a phonetic marriage.' A formal notice appeared in *The Times*:

MARRIAGES
MARAINI : ALLIATA – On Sept. 21, 1935, at Florence, FOSCO MARAINI, Sottotenente 4 Alpini, elder son of the Onorevole Antonio Maraini and Signora Yoï Maraini, to TOPAZIA ALLIATA, elder daughter of the Duca and Duchessa di Salaparuta, of Palermo.[129]

Years later, Topazia remembered her mother-in-law fondly:

... Yoï was an extremely fascinating woman: cultured, ironical and refined, she always wore precious silks embroidered by hand from oriental designs, she had a collection of jade in soft colours and she bewitched all those that knew her with her warm and sweet voice.[130]

Antonio's work as a sculptor continued to make an impression, in Italy and beyond. In May 1938, *The Times* printed a report from their Berlin Correspondent:

> *Field-Marshal Göring, the Minister President, has received from Signor Mussolini a bronze figure by the Italian sculptor Antonio Maraini, showing a kneeling warrior with shield and sword. The Duce's present was handed to the Field-Marshal to-day by Dr. Frank, one of the German Ministers who accompanied Herr Hitler to Italy. Field-Marshal Göring spoke with much appreciation of certain works of Italian sculptors when he opened the Italian Art Exhibition in Berlin last year.*[131]

In 1938, the sixth Venice Film Festival was to be dogged by accusations of political bias.

> *Owing to their dissatisfaction at, among other things, the methods adopted in allocating the various awards at the Venice International Film Festival, Mr. Neville Kearney, the British member of the jury, and Mr. Smith, the American member, who had both protested during yesterday's discussions, resigned from the jury immediately after the list of awards was published. It is understood they have both taken particular exception to the award of the Mussolini Cup, the chief prize of the festival, to the German film Olympia, on the grounds that it is a documentary and not a feature film, and therefore ineligible.*
>
> *Their action seems to have met with wide measure of approval, for in certain quarters the opinion was expressed that in making their decisions some of the jury had allowed themselves to be swayed by political motives.*
>
> *Reuter's Venice correspondent states that the Mussolini Cup was shared between the film to which objection was taken and Luciano Serra, Airman, the first film directed by Signor Vittorio Mussolini, the Duce's eldest son.*[132]

Antonio felt obliged to respond in a letter to *The Times*:

VENICE FILM AWARD
TO THE EDITOR OF THE TIMES
Sir, – As general secretary of the Biennale of Venice allow me to point out that the reason mentioned in your paper of September 2 as given by the British representative against the awarding of the Mussolini Cup to the German film Olympia because

it was documentary, is untenable owing to the fact that a precedent exists. In 1934 the same prize was given to the British film "Man of Aran" which, in spite of its length, was a documentary film of the work of man against the elements.

This is in accordance with the rules of the Cinema Festival of Venice, because the only object of the prize is that it should be given to a film showing high "artistic, intellectual, scientific, or educative value" surpassing in length "a thousand metres." (Art. 2 and 5 of the Regulations.)

With regard to the statement that the resignation of the two members of the jury "has met with a wide, measure of approval," I may state that the jury was composed of the representatives of 15 different nations, that 13 of these voted for the prizes as they were given, and only two voted against. Yours truly,

ANTONIO MARAINI, General Secretary of the Biennale.[133]

Neville Kearney felt he had to reply, and the correspondence continued in *The Times* for some time without reaching any agreement.

The War Years

By 1938, the Fascists in Italy were thoroughly in control, with all opposition being suppressed, often brutally. Antonio was by now a Member of Parliament representing the *Sindacato Fascista delle Belle Arti* (Fascist Syndicate of Fine Arts) in the *Camera dei Deputati* (Chamber of Deputies).

Fosco, Yoï and Antonio's elder son, who was now twenty-six, was strongly opposed to the Fascist regime and very disturbed by the political situation. When his father presented him with a Fascist Party membership card, the *tessera*, Fosco tore it in half and threw it away. Relations between father and son were so bad that Fosco decided to leave Italy altogether and move to Japan. He had won an international study scholarship to study the Ainu people of northern Japan and would later teach Italian at Kyoto University. He left with Topazia and their three young daughters in October 1938.

Yoï came to see them off. Later, Fosco would write:

The last inquisitive onlookers went away, the last customs officials went back to their office, but there she stayed, a small, thin, lonely figure, standing on the quayside. It grew nearly dark, and she was still there. I looked at her, and looked at her, and then I couldn't see her any more.
I never saw her again.[134]

The Second World War began when Nazi Germany invaded Poland on 1 September 1939. Italy remained neutral until June 1940 when Mussolini declared war on Britain and France. It appeared to him that the conflict would soon be over with Germany as the victor, and that his own prestige as leader would be enhanced by Italy's participation. However, Hitler frequently tended to treat Mussolini as a junior ally, often withholding details of Germany's military plans and failing to provide notice of major offensives.

The various foreign campaigns launched by Mussolini were seldom to result in lasting success, and as the months passed without a victory, the death toll continued to mount. Then the Allies invaded Sicily in July 1943 and succeeded in overcoming strong German and Italian resistance. A few days later, Allied planes bombed military and civil installations near Rome. These two events helped diminish popular support for the war throughout the country.

Mussolini was deposed and imprisoned on 25 July 1943 and a new Italian government set up, led by General Pietro Badoglio and King Victor Emmanuel III. They immediately started negotiations with the Allies with a view to ending the conflict and joining with them against Germany. The resulting Armistice was signed in secret on 3 September 1943.

Through the early years of the war, life in Florence had continued more or less as usual, although there were often serious shortages of food and power. There are very few accounts of daily life in those difficult days, but one that has survived was written by Yoï's friend Dorothy Nevile Lees. After the war, she remembered searching for fuel:

Many people probably do not know what a gazzozzolo is. Neither did I until, in recent years, during an acute fuel shortage, Marietta, invaluable household help of twenty years' standing, told me; and necessity soon taught me the use and value of these small cones which, ripening and drying, drop in due course from the cypress trees.

Fuel was hard to come by in those days, trucks and tyres were lacking to bring it into the city from outlying, often far distant, places and over roads subject to air raids at any moment. Sometimes Marietta had to queue up for even six or seven hours, in rain, wind, cold, to secure a meagre ration of six or seven pounds of inferior charcoal, damp and full of pebbles. The large pine cones, once sold so cheaply and universally in Italian fuel shops, had become scarce and costly:

gas and electricity were reduced to a minimum and finally failed entirely. The problem of keeping the kitchen fires burning, on even the most limited scale, was urgent and not easy of solution.

Then one day Marietta chanced to mention that, in childhood, her thrifty peasant mother used to send the children out to gather gazzozzoli to burn. What were gazzozzoli? Once I knew, I realised that here was an unexploited, however modest, source of supply; something to be had, for the mere taking, to meet a need; and so, from that day forward, my wanderings were accompanied by a capacious bag in which to carry home this treasure trove.

The search gave a certain zest and aim to walks in a period when, for Allied subjects in Italy, restrictions and prohibitions sought to intrude themselves at every turn.[135]

In her diary for 8 September 1943, Dorothy wrote excitedly:

A day that seemed like any other day yet ended in PEACE between the Allies and Italy!... What joy for everyone! What hope of better times, better relations between Italy and other countries from now onwards; what relief that the carnage and destruction of these years is over, and the hostilities between Italy and the Allies at an end![136]

Later that evening, she visited Yoï and Antonio at *Torre di Sopra*:

Several young Italian soldiers came in also, wild with joy, having escaped from their barracks to celebrate.

My friends saw me home before the 11 o'clock curfew. All was very quiet at the Porta Romana, the wide piazza quite deserted, and there was a heavy mist. All the houses were darkened as usual, and we met no one on the road. Instead of rejoicing and relief there was, indeed, an unwonted sense of oppression; something ominous, foreboding, in the atmosphere, and, the first brief moment of exultation over, we were already saying to one another, "How will the Germans take this? What will happen next?"[137]

After several days of total chaos came the news no one wanted to hear – the Germans had occupied Rome and were soon to occupy Florence. At midday on Saturday 11 September, a German plane flew over the city dropping leaflets. These declared that the Italians had betrayed their ally and were now to be made to pay. By the evening…

… the Germans had occupied the railway station, the radio station, telephone and other public buildings and military centres and had set big guns and stationed men at all these and on the bridges over the Arno, armed with muskets and hand bombs. Everywhere there was a sense of oppression and menace.[138]

It was to be nearly a year before the German army was to leave again. Another blow was to fall when on 16 September banner headlines in the evening paper announced the release of Mussolini from captivity. Also on the front page were instructions for all military personnel and Fascist party members to resume their posts, while "cowards and traitors" were to be punished in exemplary manner. All demonstrations of any kind were absolutely forbidden.

The situation in those days was chaotic. The people, demoralised by twenty years of fascism, political irresponsibility and subjection to tyranny, veered this way and that, without rudder or lode-star. There was no one to give a lead in the cause of freedom. Neo-Fascism, with Mussolini reinstated as pawn of the Teutonic overlords, followed at the heels of the detested Germans who were prolonging a losing struggle, at Italy's expense, on Italian soil.[139]

Small wonder then that one night someone wrote on the statue of the Italian popular hero, Giuseppe Garibaldi: *Scendi, Beppino! Sono tornati!* (Come down, Beppino! They have returned!)

In one sentence, Dorothy summed up the situation:

Now they entered and dominated: their heel was on everyone and everything; they were the law-givers – exasperated and vengeful law-givers; and, seconded by the obsequious (and despised) collaborators of the Fascist republicans who ran to and fro at their bidding, eager for favour and emoluments, a reign of terror began.[140]

Informers were everywhere, and the population gradually became more and more wary, talking to each other in whispers, or using code words. Speaking English would result in the police being informed.

During those months the hunt was up, and the game – human game – was plentiful.

There were the disbanded Italian forces, officers and men, who had scattered after the armistice, refused to take the republican oath, and had not succeeded in crossing the frontier into neutral but generously hospitable Switzerland. There were all of military age who, called to arms by the neo-fascists in subservience to the Germans, failed to respond to the call: all the liberated prisoners of war and those who were helping and hiding them; and all those who, after the fall of Fascism, had expressed themselves freely, taken an openly anti-fascist stand. There were the political refugees who had filtered back, after the 25th July from years of exile: the able-bodied men whom Germany coveted as slave-labourers: the Jews who had hitherto survived and escaped deportation and were now faced by a yet more bitter persecution, a more relentless hunting down.

Those were the months of hiding, when, with evil rampant and claiming to be all-powerful, innumerable people were hiding others or being hidden themselves. Even within one's own small circle one came in touch with, knew of, so many, so very many of such fugitives!

We English, too, were in no pleasant a position. On October 5th it was learned that on the previous evening German officers had been to the Questura [Police Headquarters] to get the list of all English and American names; and it was obvious that this boded us no good. Indeed, from that day onwards we knew no respite until the Allies entered Florence ten months later.

During these house-to-house visitations anyone, no matter who, was liable to be arrested, or seized for slave labour; carried off, entrained, and despatched to Germany, Poland or any other destination, probably to be heard of no more.[141]

One group of young men of military age took refuge inside Brunelleschi's famous dome on Florence's cathedral, the *Duomo*. They lived there for three months, with a few anxious moments, but survived safely.[142]

Yoï herself was in considerable danger. Dorothy later wrote:

An English friend of mine, married to an Italian, had incurred suspicion as unduly friendly with and helpful to her own people. Called and cross-examined by the dreaded S. S., she was destined to be delivered over to the ferocious Farinacci at Cremona and then drafted to Germany. By intervention of an Italian lawyer and the good will of the officials at the Questura, a respite was obtained on the grounds of ill health; and, to secure the benefits of this it was essential to pose as completely bed-ridden, in the hope of delaying and delaying until the Allies should arrive.

Accordingly, to render appearances yet more convincing, arrangements were made for her to be received, as an "invalid" requiring a rest cure after serious illness, in a convent. The Mother Superior made no comment, beyond asking whether she was Aryan or Jew, when I went to engage the room: and there she lay, never moving from her bed, and with the approval of the Questura, for many weeks. Her presence there was a secret from all but three or four people and to visit there was compromising: but throughout that time I was able to visit her daily without any harmful results, and my intrepid Maria also braved all risks to go daily to carry down food. [143]

Apart from that of her long-serving maid, Maria, Dorothy discreetly does not give any names, but family sources confirm that Yoï did indeed hide in the convent hospital to avoid deportation.

As the weeks went by, conditions in the city worsened, with water and food being very difficult to obtain. The Allies reached Florence in August and a battle for the city began. By this time, the German army had destroyed all but one of the bridges over the Arno and laid waste a wide area around the *Ponte Vecchio*. Finally, the city was liberated, although still under fire from the German positions on the northern hills. On Monday 14 August 1944, *The Times* reported that Florence was finally free:

Florence is free again. The Germans evacuated the northern bank at 2.30 a.m., on Friday, and at about daylight they blew up bridges over the Mugnone, a tributary of the Arno which forms the northern boundary of the city. The glad news was first made known to the southern bank by the ringing of the bell in the tall tower of the Palazzo Vecchio, and soon after people were seen on the northern Lungarno shouting: "Come over. We're free." [144]

Yoï was now able to leave the hospital, return home, and begin to pick up the pieces of her life. But the deprivations of the last few years had taken a severe toll, and her health, which had never been particularly good, was now to let her down. She died on Tuesday 31 October 1944 in her garden at *Torre di Sopra*. She was sixty-seven years old.

She is buried near the Church of *San Miniato al Monte*, overlooking her adopted city of Florence, where she had lived for nearly half her life.

Afterwards

After the war, Antonio remained at *Torre di Sopra*, where he led a secluded life. To a large extent, he retired from both public life and his work as a sculptor, although he did carve a headstone for Yoï's grave. He also accepted the presidency of the *Accademia del Disegno di Firenze*.

Yoï's elder son, Fosco, became well known as a photographer, anthropologist, ethnologist, writer, mountaineer and academic, publishing a number of books on Tibet and Japan. Dorothy's son, David Lees, became a photographer for *Life* magazine.

The Australian writer Geoffrey Dutton stayed in Florence in 1953. In his autobiography, *Out in the Open,* he recalled visiting *Torre di Sopra*:

> *Grato Maraini looked like a great blond condottiero in a Renaissance painting; he lived with his father in an immense villa. The two men never spoke, and at meals sat at opposite ends of a table the length of a cricket pitch, reading their separate copies of the London Times.* [145]

Dacia Maraini, who is Yoï's granddaughter, has memories of accompanying her grandfather Antonio on his Sunday walk to the cemetery to visit Yoï's grave. She remembers him as being always critical and lacking in affection to his grandchildren:

> *He always told me that I was ugly and that I could never be like my grandmother, the beautiful Yoï, who had eyes "hollowed with the chisel" and for him as a sculptor this was the greatest compliment.* [146]

After Antonio's death in 1963, *Torre di Sopra* was divided between Fosco and Grato. They both died in 2004. Four years later, on 18 March 2008, the firm of *Pandolfini* held an auction of the contents in Florence, including the furniture, many items of sculpture by Antonio, and photographs by Fosco. The subtitle of the auction catalogue, *Memorie di una Famiglia (Memories of a Family)*, seems appropriate to mark the ending of the life that Yoï had made for herself and her family in her adopted country of Italy.

Appendix 1 –
Published works by Yoï Maraini

A Year of Strangers	Yoï Pawlowska	Duckworth	1911
Those That Dream	Yoï Pawlowska	Duckworth	1912
A Child Went Forth	Yoï Pawlowska	Duckworth	1914
In a Grain of Sand	Yoï Maraini	W. Collins	1922
Little Dressmakers in Love	Yoï Maraini	Methuen	1925

Articles for several English periodicals: in particular, the *Anglo-Italian Review*, the *Architectural Review*, and the *Saturday Review*.

Appendix 2 – Major works by Antonio Maraini

Two panels: *Music mourning the death of the Master* and *Music that outlives the Master*, Puccini's tomb, Torre del Lago	1926
Bronze panels for the front door of the *Basilica di San Paolo fuori le Mura* (the Basilica of St. Paul Outside the Walls) in Rome	1929 – 1931
Panels for the spiral staircase of the Vatican Museums	1932
Panels for the *Arengario* (orator's podium) in the Piazza Vittoria, Brescia	1932

Notes

1   For a detailed account of the life of Andrew Crosse, see Wright, Brian, *Andrew Crosse and the mite that shocked the world*, Matador, 2015

2   Crosse, Cornelia (Mrs Andrew Crosse), *Memorials of Andrew Crosse the Electrician,* 1857, p. 60

3   Tweedie, Mrs. Alec, *Mrs Andrew Crosse, The Queen, The Lady's newspaper*, 16 March 1895

4   Haggard, H. Rider, *The Days of My Life*, Volume I (1926)

5   Westminster School Register, 1892

6   Crosse, A. F., *Round About the Carpathians*, Blackwood, 1878, p. 13

7   *ibid.* p. 291

8   Announcement in the *Pall Mall Gazette*, Friday 6 Oct 1876

9   *The Collected Correspondence and London Notebooks of Joseph Haydn*, H. C. Robbins Landon, 1959, p. 151

10   Armour, Gabriella (née Crosse), *Far Away and Long Ago* (unpublished memoir)

11   *ibid.* p. 355

12   Crosse, Cornelia (Mrs Andrew Crosse), *Red Letter days of my Life,* 1892, Vol. II p. 258

13   Armour, Gabriella, *op. cit.*

14   Crosse, A. F., *op. cit.*, pp. 372-4

15   *ibid.* p. 365

16   Armour, Gabriella, *op. cit.*

17   Pawlowska, Yoï, *A Child went Forth*, 1914

18   *ibid.* p. 12
19   *ibid.* p. 35
20   *ibid.* pp. 37-38
21   *ibid.* p. 44
22   *ibid.* pp. 150-151
23   Armour, Gabriella, *op. cit.*
24   Pawlowska, Yoï, *op. cit.,* p. 177
25   *The Times*, 4 November 1889
26   *The Times*, 27 August 1890
27   Tweedie, Mrs. Alec, *op. cit.*
28   http://www.britannica.com/EBchecked/topic/239545/Sir-Edmund-Gosse
29   Outward passenger lists, 23 January 1891
30   Inward passenger lists, 11 April 1892
31   Crosse, A. F., letter written from Tállya, 10 May 1892
32   Armour, Gabriella, *op. cit.*
33   *ibid.*
34   *ibid.*
35   Outward passenger lists, 2 June 1892
36   *The Times*, 19 November 1892
37   Announcement in the *Bristol Mercury,* Tuesday 22 Oct 1895
38   Tweedie, Mrs. Alec, *op. cit*
39   *The Times*, 5 Mar 1895
40   *South Wales Daily Post*, 27th November 1895
41   *Llanelly Mercury*, 21 April 1896, quoted in *Parc Howard, From Mansion to Museum*, by William & Benita Rees, published on CD, from which the above details of the Buckley family are taken.
42   *The Times*, 15 December 1887
43   Inward passenger lists, 1 August 1896
44   *Llanelly & County Guardian*, 1 June 1899, quoted in *Parc Howard, From Mansion to Museum*, by William & Benita Rees, published on CD
45   *The Times*, 8 May 1901
46   *The Times*, 10 May 1901
47   *The Times*, 27 May 1901
48   *London Gazette*, 11 March 1902

49   *The Times*, 25 December 1902

50   British Patent No. 269 (1909)

51   Outward passenger lists, 3 July 1909

52   Buckley, E. C., *Statement of Facts*, 1912. Unless otherwise identified, all quoted passages in this chapter are from this booklet. The copy in the British Library is annotated by Edward Heron-Allen, Yoï's solicitor.

53   Pawlowska, Yoï, *A Year of Strangers*, 1911

54   *The Times*, 8 February 1910

55   Pawlowska, Yoï, *A Year of Strangers*, 1911, p. 59

56   *ibid.* p. 66

57   *ibid.* p. 71

58   *ibid.* p. 72

59   *ibid.* p. 73

60   *ibid.* p. 73

61   *ibid.* p. 77

62   *ibid.* p. 89

63   *ibid.* p. 102

64   *The Times*, 17 December 1910

65   *The Times*, 5 January 1911

66   *The Times*, 5 April 1911

67   *The Times*, 8 May 1918

68   Pawlowska, Yoï, *A Year of Strangers*, 1911, Introduction

69   *ibid.* p. 147

70   Dunn, Richard M., *Geoffrey Scott and the Berenson Circle*, 1998, p.130

71   Bardazzi, Francesca, *Antonio Maraini Scultore*, 1984, p. 4

72   Buckley, E. C, *Statement of Facts*, 1912, pp. 3-5

73   *Rhythm*, No. XI with Literary Supplement, December 1912

74   *Rhythm*, No. XIII, February 1913, pp. 409-411

75   *The Times*, 29 May 1914

76   *Punch, or The London Charivari*, Vol. 146, 24 June 1914, p. 29

77   Maraini, Yoï, *Eleonora Duse,* in *The Saturday Review*, 9 June 1923

78   *ibid.*

79   Maraini, Yoï, *Fear under the Stars,* in *The Saturday Review,* 5 August 1922

80 Maraini, Yoï, *letters to Emilio Cecchi*, in the Archivio Contemperaneo A. Bonsanti, Florence

81 *ibid.*

82 *ibid.*

83 *ibid.*

84 *ibid.*

85 *ibid.*

86 *ibid.*

87 *ibid.*

88 British Patent No. 269 (1909)

89 British Patent No 11,375 (1910)

90 Crosse, A. F., *Journal of the Chemical, Metallurgical and Mineralogical Society of S. Africa*, XXI 126/2

91 *The Times*, 17 August 1921

92 Maraini, Yoï, *In a Grain of Sand*, 1922, Introduction

93 *Llanelly Guardian*, 25 August 1923, quoted in *Parc Howard, From Mansion to Museum*, by William & Benita Rees, published on CD

94 Heron-Allen, Edward, *Holiday Journals: Rome and Florence 1923*, unpublished manuscript, West Sussex Record Office, Heron-Allen MS. 1/2/1/22, pp.15-21

95 *The Times*, 4 January 1924

96 Smith, Denis Mack, *Mussolini*, 1981, pp.111-2

97 Maraini, Yoï, *A Talk with Mussolini*, *The Saturday Review*, 5 April 1924

98 For more details of Dorothy Nevile Lees' life and work, see Sborgi, Ilaria B., *Behind the Mask: Dorothy Nevile Lees' Florentine Contribution to Edward Gordon Craig's "New Theatre"*, published in *Otherness, Anglo-American Women in 19th and 20th Century Florence* (2001)

99 *Letters of Yoï Maraini*, D. N. Lees Collection, Houghton Library, Harvard University, *No. 3619*

100 Maraini, Fosco, *Case, amori, universi*, 1999, p. 10 (my translation)

101 Maraini, Yoï, *A Talk with Aldous Huxley, The Bermondsey Book*, Vol. III No 3, June 1926, p.76

102 Maraini, Yoï, *Letter to Pinker*, 1925, Huxley papers (M0107), Department of Special Collections, Stanford University Libraries

103 Maraini, Yoï, *A Tuscan Farmhouse*, in *The Architectural Review*, Vol. 64, September 1928, pp.102-105

104 *The Times*, 21 October 1926

105 *South Wales Press*, 12 January 1927, quoted in *Parc Howard, From Mansion to Museum*, by William & Benita Rees, published on CD

106 *The Times*, 4 May 1928

107 *Letters of Yoï Maraini*, D. N. Lees Collection, Houghton Library, Harvard University, *No. 3641*

108 *British Journal of Nursing*, November 1928

109 *Letters of Yoï Maraini*, D. N. Lees Collection, Houghton Library, Harvard University, *No. 3884*

110 *Letters of Yoï Maraini*, D. N. Lees Collection, Houghton Library, Harvard University, *No. 3649*

111 *Llanelly Mercury*, 27 June 1929

112 *Letters of Yoï Maraini*, D. N. Lees Collection, Houghton Library, Harvard University, *No. 3878a*

113 *Letters of Yoï Maraini*, D. N. Lees Collection, Houghton Library, Harvard University, *No. 3878b*

114 Maraini, Fosco, *Case, amori, universi*, 1999, p. 178 (my translation)

115 *ibid.*, pp. 179-180

116 Maraini, Yoï; *The Modern Italians (Decorative Arts and Crafts in Italy related to "the present exhibition at Burlington House")* in the *Architectural Review* Vol. 67, January – June 1930; pp. 101-104

117 *Letters of Yoï Maraini*, D. N. Lees Collection, Houghton Library, Harvard University, *No. 3674*

118 *Letters of Yoï Maraini*, D. N. Lees Collection, Houghton Library, Harvard University, *No. 3715*

119 *Letters of Yoï Maraini*, D. N. Lees Collection, Houghton Library, Harvard University, *No. 3881*

120 *Letters of Yoï Maraini*, D. N. Lees Collection, Houghton Library, Harvard University, *No. 3890*

121 Memorial to Ifor Buckley, Holy Trinity Church, Felinfoel

122 *Letters of Yoï Maraini*, D. N. Lees Collection, Houghton Library, Harvard University, *No. 3691*

123 *ibid.*

124 *Letters of Yoï Maraini*, D. N. Lees Collection, Houghton Library,

Harvard University, *No. 3710*

125 *Letters of Yoï Maraini*, D. N. Lees Collection, Houghton Library, Harvard University, *No. 3713a*

126 *The Times*, 12 May 1934

127 *TIME Magazine*, 2 July 1934

128 *Letters of Yoï Maraini*, D. N. Lees Collection, Houghton Library, Harvard University, *No. 3723*

129 *The Times*, 25 September 1935

130 Dacia Maraini, *Yoï Pawlowska scrittrice, mia nonna (1877-1944)*, published in *Viaggio e Scrittura, le Stranieri nell'Italia dell'Ottocento*, (1988), p. 176 (my translation)

131 *The Times*, 13 May 1938

132 *The Times*, 2 September 1938

133 *The Times*, 17 September 1938

134 Maraini, Fosco, *Secret Tibet*

135 Lees, D. N., *Tribute to a Gazzozzolo*, article in the *Christian Science Monitor*, 5 September 1947

136 Lees, D. N., *Life Goes On*, unpublished MS in the Archivio Contemporaneo A. Bonsanti, Florence, p. 200

137 *ibid.*, p. 201

138 *ibid.*, p. 203

139 *ibid.*, p. 206

140 *ibid.*, p. 210

141 *ibid.*, pp. 231-2

142 *ibid.*, pp. 292-3

143 *ibid.*, pp. 291-2

144 *The Times*, 14 August 1944

145 Dutton, Geoffrey, *Out in the Open*, 1994, p. 197

146 Dacia Maraini, *Yoï Pawlowska scrittrice, mia nonna (1877-1944)*, published in *Viaggio e Scrittura, le Stranieri nell'Italia dell'Ottocento*, (1988), p. 175 (my translation)

Index